The best of Mrs BEETON'S Easy Entertaining

The best of Mrs Beeton's Easy Entertaining

WEIDENFELD & NICOLSON

First published in 2006 by the Orion Publishing Group Ltd
5 Upper St Martin's Lane
London
WC2H 9EA

Designed by seagulls and cbdesign
Index prepared by Chris Bell
Produced by Omnipress Ltd, Eastbourne
Printed and bound in the UK by
CPI Mackays, Chatham ME5 8TD

Contents

Soups, Starters & Snacks

Vibrant flavours to stimulate the palate without dulling the appetite.

CHANTILLY SOUP

Use fresh peas to make this simple soup. The best pods are plump and well filled without being too tightly packed.

30 ml / 2 tbsp butter
2 onions, finely chopped
1.4 kg / 3 lb peas in the pod
(about 675 g / 1½ lb when shelled)
1 small bunch of parsley, chopped
1.5 litres / 2¾ pints Chicken Stock (page 187)
salt and pepper

Melt the butter in a large saucepan. Add the onions and cook over gentle heat for 10 minutes until soft but not coloured.

Meanwhile shell the peas, reserving about 6 of the best pods. Stir the peas and parsley into the pan and add the stock, with salt and pepper to taste. Wash the pods and add them to the pan.

Bring the stock to simmering point (see Mrs Beeton's Tip) and cook for about 20 minutes, or until the peas are very soft. Remove the pods.

Purée the soup in a blender or food processor, or rub through a sieve into a clean pan. Bring to just below boiling point and serve at once.

SERVES SIX

MRS BEETON'S TIP

Do not allow the soup to boil after the peas have been added, or you will spoil the colour.

FRESH ASPARAGUS SOUP

450 g / 1 lb fresh asparagus
salt and white pepper
1.4 litres / 2½ pints Chicken Stock (page 187)
50 g / 2 oz butter
1 small onion, chopped
50 g / 2 oz plain flour
1 egg yolk
150 ml / ¼ pint double cream,
single cream or fromage frais,
according to preference

Cut off the asparagus tips and put them in a saucepan. Add salted water to cover, bring to the boil, then simmer for about 5 minutes or until tender. Drain the tips and set aside.

Slice the asparagus stalks and cook them in 600 ml / 1 pint of the stock until tender (they will take up to 15 minutes). Purée in a blender or food processor, or rub through a sieve.

Melt the butter in a large saucepan, add the onion and fry over gentle heat for about 10 minutes until soft. Stir in the flour and cook for 1 minute, stirring constantly. Gradually add the remaining stock, stirring until the mixture boils and thickens. Stir in the asparagus purée, with salt and pepper to taste. Reheat.

In a small bowl, mix the egg yolk with the cream. Stir a little of the hot soup into the egg mixture, mix well, then add the contents of the bowl to the soup, stirring over low heat until the mixture thickens slightly. Add the reserved asparagus tips and heat through without boiling. Serve at once.

SERVES SIX

CUCUMBER AND YOGURT SOUP

Low in calories, this is the ideal soup for a summer lunch party.

15 ml / 1 tbsp butter or light olive oil
1 small onion, finely chopped
½ large cucumber, peeled and cut into 5-mm / ¼-inch dice
450 ml / ¾ pint plain yogurt
250 ml / 8 fl oz Chicken Stock (page 187) or well-flavoured Vegetable Stock (page 188)
grated rind and juice of ½ lemon
10 ml / 2 tsp finely chopped mint
salt and pepper
mint sprigs to garnish

Melt the butter in a saucepan, add the onion and cucumber and cook over very gentle heat for 8–10 minutes. Leave to cool.

Whisk the yogurt in a bowl until smooth. Add the onion mixture with the stock. Stir in the lemon rind and juice, with the mint. Add salt and pepper to taste. Cover the bowl and chill for several hours. Serve in chilled bowls, garnished with mint sprigs.

SERVES THREE TO FOUR

MRS BEETON'S TIP

Omit the stock to make a creamy dip, ideal for serving with breadsticks, crudites or crisps.

CARROT SOUP

Grating the vegetables speeds up the cooking time, making this an ideal soup for those occasions when time is short.

600 ml / 1 pint Chicken Stock (page 187), or Vegetable Stock (page 188)
3 carrots, grated
1 onion, finely chopped
1 potato, grated
25 g / 1 oz butter
25 g / 1 oz plain flour
300 ml / ½ pint milk
salt and pepper
grated nutmeg

Combine the stock, carrots, onion and potato in a saucepan. Bring to the boil, lower the heat and simmer gently for about 15 minutes, or until the vegetables are tender.

Meanwhile melt the butter in a separate saucepan, add the flour and cook for 1 minute. Gradually stir in the milk, then add the stock and vegetables. Heat, stirring constantly, until the mixture boils and thickens. Add salt, pepper and nutmeg to taste. Serve at once, with triangles of hot toast, if liked.

SERVES FOUR

VARIATION

- **Carrot and Orange Soup** Cut the carrot into matchstick strips and use 1 parsnip, cut into similar strips, instead of the potato. Use 900 ml / 1½ pints stock and add 60 ml / 4 tbsp fresh orange juice. Omit the milk and do not thicken the soup.

PUMPKIN SOUP

25 g / 1 oz butter
1 onion, finely chopped
1 garlic clove, crushed
1 kg / 2¼ lb pumpkin, peeled, seeded and cubed
1.5 litres / 2¾ pints Chicken Stock (page 187), or Vegetable Stock (page 188)
5 ml / 1 tsp ground coriander seeds
5 ml / 1 tsp ground cinnamon
2.5 ml / ½ tsp ground cumin
salt and pepper
150 ml / ¼ pint whipping cream or fromage frais

Melt the butter in a large saucepan, add the onion and garlic and cook over gentle heat for 10 minutes until soft but not coloured.

Add the pumpkin cubes, stock and spices and season with salt and pepper to taste. Bring to the boil, lower the heat and simmer for about 30 minutes or until the pumpkin is tender.

Purée the soup in a blender or food processor, or rub through a sieve into a clean pan. Taste and add more salt and pepper if required. The soup should be quite spicy. Reheat without boiling.

Whip the cream, if using. Ladle the soup into individual bowls and top each portion with a spoonful of whipped cream or fromage frais.

SERVES SIX

VARIATION

- **Pumpkin and Apple Soup** Omit the coriander and cumin. Add 2 peeled, cored and sliced cooking apples with the pumpkin. Continue as above, then stir in a little sugar to taste when reheated. The sweetness should just balance the tang of the apples. Serve as above.

CAULIFLOWER SOUP

1 large cauliflower
25 g / 1 oz butter
1 onion, finely chopped
900 ml / 1½ pints milk
salt and pepper
2 egg yolks
150 ml / ¼ pint single cream
50 g / 2 oz flaked almonds, toasted

Steam the cauliflower whole for 20–30 minutes until tender. Cut it into florets, reserving any leaves or tender stem.

Melt the butter in a small frying pan. Add the onion and cook over gentle heat for about 10 minutes, until soft but not coloured. Purée the cauliflower and the onion mixture with 250 ml / 8 fl oz of the milk in a blender or food processor, then rub through a fine sieve into a clean pan.

Stir the remaining milk into the pan, with salt and pepper to taste. Heat the soup to just below boiling point, then lower the heat so that it barely simmers. In a small bowl, mix the egg yolks with the cream. Stir a little of the hot soup into the egg mixture, mix well, then add the contents of the bowl to the soup, stirring over low heat until it thickens. Serve at once, topped with toasted almonds.

SERVES FOUR

MRS BEETON'S TIP

To make a quick cauliflower soup, break the vegetable into florets and place in a saucepan with 1 diced potato and 1 chopped onion. Add 600 ml / 1 pint chicken stock and bring to the boil. Simmer, covered for 30 minutes, then purée. Add 300 ml / ½ pint milk and seasoning to taste. Heat without boiling.

YELLOW SPLIT PEA SOUP

30 ml / 2 tbsp oil
6 rindless streaky bacon rashers, chopped
1 large onion, finely chopped
100 g / 4 oz yellow split peas, soaked overnight in water to cover
2 litres / 3½ pints Chicken Stock (page 187) or Vegetable Stock (page 188)
60 ml / 4 tbsp chopped celery leaves
2 parsley sprigs
2 bay leaves
5 ml / ½ tsp chopped summer savory or 2.5 ml / ½ tsp dried savory
salt and pepper

Heat the oil in a large saucepan. Add the bacon and onion and fry for 10 minutes over gentle heat, until the onion is soft but not coloured.

Drain the split peas and add them to the pan with the stock, celery leaves, parsley, bay leaves and savory. Add salt and pepper to taste. Bring to the boil, lower the heat and simmer for about 2 hours, or until the peas are very tender. If the soup becomes too thick, add water or extra stock.

Remove the parsley sprigs and bay leaves. Serve the soup as it is, or purée in a blender or food processor. Alternatively, rub through a sieve into a clean pan. Reheat, stirring frequently to prevent the soup from sticking to the pan, and serve at once.

SERVES FOUR TO SIX

VARIATION

- **Pea and Ham Soup** Save the stock when boiling a joint of ham or bacon as it makes delicious split pea soup. Omit the streaky bacon and do not add seasoning until the soup is cooked.

PRESSURE COOKER TIP

It is not necessary to soak the split peas if the soup is to be made in a pressure cooker. Fry the bacon and onion in the oil in the open cooker. Add the split peas and herbs as in the recipe above, but reduce the amount of stock to 1 litre / 1¾ pints. Put the lid on the cooker and bring to 15 lb pressure. Cook for 12 minutes. Reduce pressure slowly, then continue as described above, adding more stock to adjust the consistency as desired.

VICHYSOISSE

A simple soup which can be served hot, but tastes even better chilled.

25 g / 1 oz butter
450 g / 1 lb leeks, white parts only, trimmed, sliced and washed
2 onions, chopped
450 g / 1 lb potatoes, cubed
900 ml / 1½ pints Chicken Stock (page 187)
salt and pepper
150 ml / ¼ pint milk
150 ml / ¼ pint single cream
snipped chives to garnish

Melt the butter in a saucepan, add the leeks, onions and potatoes and fry gently for 10 minutes without browning. Stir in the stock, with salt and pepper to taste. Bring to the boil, lower the heat and simmer for about 30 minutes or until the vegetables are soft.

Purée the mixture in a blender or food processor, or press through a sieve into a bowl. Cool quickly, then stir in the milk and cream. Add more salt and pepper if required. Cover and chill for 4–6 hours. Serve in chilled individual bowls, sprinkled with chives.

SERVES FOUR TO SIX

FRENCH ONION SOUP

75 g / 3 oz butter, plus extra for toast
6 onions, about 575 g / 1¼ lb, thinly sliced
1 litre / 1¾ pints well-flavoured Vegetable Stock (page 188)
30 ml / 2 tbsp dry white wine
salt and pepper
6 slices of French bread
50 g / 2 oz Gruyère, grated

Melt the butter in a large heavy-bottomed saucepan. Add the onions and cook slowly, turning occasionally, for at least 30 minutes, or until golden brown.

Stir in the Vegetable Stock and white wine. Bring to the boil, lower the heat and cover the pan, then simmer for about 1 hour, or until the onions are quite soft. Add salt and pepper to taste.

Toast the French bread, spread it with butter and top with grated cheese. Pour the soup into individual bowls, float a slice of toast on each, and brown the cheese under a preheated hot grill or in a very hot oven.

SERVES FOUR

MRS BEETON'S TIP

Sprinkle 2.5 ml / ½ tsp sugar over the onions while browning them in the butter. This will encourage the browning process. The wine may be omitted from the soup, and a little brandy added just before floating the toast on top.

SMOKED HADDOCK CHOWDER

450 g / 1 lb smoked haddock fillet, skinned
750 ml / 1¼ pints milk
50 g / 2 oz butter
1 small onion, finely chopped
100 g / 4 oz mushrooms, finely chopped
40 g / 1½ oz plain flour
250 ml / 8 fl oz single cream
freshly ground black pepper

Put the haddock fillets into a saucepan with the milk and heat to simmering point. Simmer for about 10 minutes until just tender. Drain the fish, reserving the cooking liquid, remove the skin and shred the fish lightly.

Melt the butter in a clean pan, add the onion and mushrooms and fry gently for about 10 minutes until soft. Do not allow the onion to colour.

Stir in the flour and cook for 1 minute, stirring constantly. Gradually add the fish-flavoured milk, stirring until smooth. Bring to the boil, lower the heat and simmer until thickened.

Off the heat, add the cream and the shredded haddock. Return the pan to the heat and warm through gently. Do not allow the soup to boil after adding the cream. Top with a generous grinding of black pepper and serve at once.

SERVES FOUR TO SIX

MRS BEETON'S TIP

Reserve a few perfect mushrooms for a garnish if liked. Slice them thinly and sprinkle a few slices on top of each portion of soup. It is not necessary to cook the mushrooms.

FISH BALL SOUP

50 g / 2 oz fresh root ginger, peeled and finely chopped
1 spring onion, finely chopped
15 ml / 1 tbsp dry sherry
1 egg white
225 g / 8 oz firm white fish fillet, skinned and cut into pieces
25 ml / 5 tsp cornflour
salt
25 g / 1 oz lard, softened
snipped chives to garnish

CHINESE CHICKEN STOCK
2 chicken quarters
1 onion, thickly sliced
1 large carrot, thickly sliced
1 celery stick, thickly sliced
1 thin slice of fresh root ginger
5 ml / 1 tsp dry sherry

Make the stock. Put the chicken quarters in a heavy-bottomed saucepan. Add 2 litres / 3½ pints water and bring to the boil. Skim, lower the heat, cover and simmer for 1½ hours. Remove the chicken from the stock and set aside for use in another recipe.

Add the vegetables to the stock, cover and simmer for 20 minutes. Stir in the root ginger and sherry, with salt to taste. Remove the lid and simmer for 10 minutes more. Strain the stock into a clean saucepan, making it up to 1.25 litres / 2½ pints with water if necessary. Skim off any fat on the surface and set aside.

To make the fish balls, sieve the root ginger and spring onion into a bowl containing 75 ml / 5 tbsp water. Stir briskly. Alternatively, process the root ginger, spring onion and water in a blender or food processor. Strain the liquid into a clean bowl, discarding any solids. Add a further 75 ml / 5 tbsp water to the liquid, with the sherry and the egg white. Whisk until smooth.

FREEZER TIP

The shaped fish balls may be frozen before cooking. Open freeze them on a baking sheet lined with freezer film, then pack in polythene bags when firm. Cook from frozen in soup. Alternatively, the fish balls may be deep fried or stir fried.

Place the fish in a basin or large mortar and pound it to a paste. Alternatively, purée the fish in a food processor. Transfer 15 ml / 1 tbsp of the sherry mixture to a shallow bowl and add the fish. Stir in the cornflour, salt and lard, and mix thoroughly so that the ingredients bind together. The mixture should be soft and malleable; add more of the sherry mixture as necessary.

Form the fish mixture into balls about 4 cm / 1½ inches in diameter and drop them into a large pan of cold water. Bring the water to the boil, lower the heat and simmer until the fish balls float. Remove with a slotted spoon.

Bring the pan of Chinese chicken stock to the boil. Drop in the fish balls and heat through for 1–2 minutes. Serve immediately, garnished with the chives.

SERVES SIX

SIMPLE FRUIT STARTERS

Light fruit starters are ideal for lunch or summer dinners. Some are also appropriate for the canapé tray.

Avocado Avocado must be ripe but not mushy. Unripe fruit is hard, bitter and has a poor flavour. Test by gently pressing the outside of the avocado: it should give slightly, feeling tender but not soft enough to be able to compress the flesh. Avoid fruit which is very hard as it may never ripen. If the avocado feels firm but not hard, leave it in a warm room for a day or two until it feels tender. Soft avocados are perfectly suitable for making dips; however, very soft fruit with loose skin which may be dented or bruised should be avoided as the flesh will probably be blackened and stringy.

Serve avocado very plain, with a vinaigrette dressing, or use it in simple salads, with leafy vegetables or tomato. Chunks of avocado, wrapped in bacon and grilled, may be served 'en brochette'; skewered as miniature kebabs or offered on cocktail sticks with pre-dinner drinks.

Banana Thickly sliced, wrapped in bacon and grilled, banana may be placed on cocktail sticks to serve with drinks.

Citrus Fruit Grapefruit is an old favourite, especially when halved and sprinkled with sugar well in advance of serving, so that the fruit is very juicy; or combined with orange in a simple cocktail. To prepare the fruit, cut it in half and use a serrated knife or grapefruit knife to loosen the flesh from the shell, then cut between the segments and remove any central core of pith and membrane.

Dates Fresh dates may be stoned and filled with soft cheese for serving with canapés.

Figs Fresh figs are delicious with Parma ham or with soft cheese – particularly goat's cheese. Peel the figs thinly, then cut them almost through into quarters, opening out the segments, flower-fashion, on individual plates. Serve with freshly ground black pepper.

MELON BOATS

1 large ripe melon, cut into 6–8 segments
1 lemon or lime, sliced
sherry or ginger wine (optional)

Using a sharp knife, slice between the melon skin and flesh on each segment to free the flesh but do not remove it. Cut the flesh across into bite-size sections. Gently ease the first row of chunks forward, then move the next row back. Continue moving neighbouring rows in this fashion so that all the pieces are staggered attractively. Three rows are the typical number in melon wedges.

Cut into the centre of each lemon or lime slice, then twist each slice and use a cocktail stick to secure the twists in the melon boats. Sprinkle each portion with sherry or ginger wine, if liked. Serve lightly chilled.

SERVES SIX TO EIGHT

MELON WITH PARMA HAM

This simple starter is always popular.

1 ripe green-fleshed melon, halved lengthways
12 slices of Parma ham

Cut the melon flesh into 16 sticks, each measuring about 7.5 x 2 cm / 3 x 1 inch and roll in the Parma ham. Alternatively, arrange the ham and melon separately on individual plates.

SERVES FOUR

MIXED HORS D'OEUVRE

A selection of complementary prepared and dressed ingredients for sampling in small portions.

Artichoke Bottoms or Hearts Fresh, cooked and prepared or canned, these may be served plain with an oil-based dressing.

Cheese Fine slices of Gruyère, Gouda or other mild, and not too rich, cheese may be included.

Cooked Meats and Poultry Ham, roast beef, smoked poultry, salami and other cured meats should be served finely sliced and attractively arranged.

Eggs Hard-boiled and halved, quartered or sliced. These may be dressed with Mayonnaise (page 197) or stuffed and garnished. Quail's eggs, smoked or plain, are ideal for hors d'oeuvre when accompanied by salt for dipping. Pickled eggs may also be used.

Tomatoes Take advantage of the different types but always select for flavour; serve with an oil-based dressing. Plum tomatoes may be sliced or quartered lengthways. Mix red and yellow cherry tomatoes. See page 38 for simple tomato salads.

Vegetable Salads Keep these simple, dressing plain well-prepared vegetables and allowing them to marinate. Suitable candidates include grated carrots with a little spring onion, finely sliced cucumber, tiny new potatoes cooked in their skins and shredded fennel or celery. Grill, peel and slice the flesh of red or green peppers for a delicious addition. Button mushrooms marinated in olive oil garlic, seasoning and lemon juice may be added to the hors d'oeuvre tray.

GARLIC AND HERB BREAD

Garlic and herb butter may be prepared using one or more herbs. When mixing herbs, balance strong and mild types. Although dried herbs may be used, fresh ones give a superior flavour. Parsley is the classic partner of garlic.

100 g / 4 oz butter, softened
1 or 2 cloves garlic, crushed
45 ml / 3 tbsp chopped parsley
5 ml / 1 tsp chopped fresh thyme or
2.5 ml / ½ tsp dried thyme
salt and pepper
1 French baguette

Beat the butter until creamy in a small bowl. Add the herbs and garlic, beating until well combined. Add salt to taste and a small pinch of pepper.

Use at once, spreading between the not-quite-cut-through slices of a French baguette, wrapping the baguette in foil and heating in a hot oven for 10 minutes; or press into small pots, tapping the pots while filling to knock out all the air. Cover with foil and refrigerate until required. Use within 2 days.

MAKES 1 BAGUETTE

POTTED SALMON

450 g / 1 lb cold cooked salmon, skinned and boned
salt and pepper
pinch of cayenne pepper
pinch of ground mace
anchovy essence
50 g / 2 oz softened clarified butter, plus extra for sealing (see Mrs Beeton's Tip, page 165)

Pound the salmon flesh in a mortar or process roughly in a blender or food processor. Add salt, pepper, cayenne, mace and anchovy essence to taste. Blend in the softened clarified butter thoroughly.

Rub the mixture through a fine sieve into a bowl. Turn into small pots. Cover with a layer of clarified butter and refrigerate until the butter is firm.

MAKES ABOUT 450 g / 1 lb

FRIED WHITING

25–50 g / 1–2 oz plain flour
salt and pepper
2 eggs
50 g / 2 oz dried white breadcrumbs for coating
12 small whiting fillets
oil for deep frying
150 ml / ¼ pint Tartare Sauce (page 195) to serve

Mix the flour with salt and pepper on a large plate. Beat the eggs in a shallow bowl. Spread out the breadcrumbs on a sheet of foil. Coat each whiting fillet first in flour, then in egg and finally in breadcrumbs. Roll up the fillets and secure with a skewer or wooden cocktail stick.

Put the oil for frying into a deep wide pan. Heat the oil to 180–190°C / 350–375°F or until a cube of bread added to the oil browns in 30 seconds.

Carefully lower the whiting rolls into the hot oil and fry for 3–5 minutes. Drain on absorbent kitchen paper and serve on a warmed platter. Hand the Tartare Sauce separately.

SERVES SIX

PRAWN COCKTAIL

4 lettuce leaves, shredded
225 g / 8 oz peeled cooked prawns
75 ml / 5 tbsp Mayonnaise (page 197)
15 ml / 1 tbsp tomato purée
few drops of Tabasco sauce
5 ml / 1 tsp chilli vinegar or tarragon vinegar (optional)
4 whole cooked prawns to garnish

Place a little shredded lettuce on the base of 4 glass dishes. Put the prawns on top. Mix the Mayonnaise with the tomato puree and add a few drops of Tabasco sauce. Stir in the vinegar, if liked.

Spoon the Mayonnaise mixture over the prawns and garnish each dish with a whole cooked prawn, preferably in the shell. Serve with brown bread and butter, if liked.

SERVES FOUR

VARIATIONS

- **Avocado Ritz** Serve the prawns and Mayonnaise on avocado halves. Cut the avocados in half and remove the stones just before topping and serving. If there is likely to be any delay, brush the avocado flesh with lemon juice to prevent discoloration.
- **Prawn and Horseradish Cocktail** Omit the Tabasco sauce and vinegar from the recipe above and add 5 ml / 1 tsp grated fresh horseradish or 15 ml / 1 tbsp Horseradish Sauce (page 198).

SARDINE CASSOLETTES

3 large slices of stale bread, each about 2 cm / ½ inch thick
oil for shallow frying
65 g / 2½ oz canned sardines in oil, drained
15 ml / 1 tbsp Greek yogurt
15 ml / 1 tbsp tomato purée
salt and pepper
few drops of lemon juice
10 ml / 2 tsp grated Parmesan cheese
watercress sprigs to garnish

Set the oven at 180°C / 350°F / gas 4. Using a 5-cm / 2-inch biscuit cutter, stamp out 8–10 rounds from the bread. Mark an inner circle on each bread round, using a 3.5-cm/ 1½-inch cutter, but do not cut right through.

Heat the oil in a large frying pan, add the bread rounds and fry until lightly browned on both sides, turning once. Remove the rounds with a slotted spoon and drain on absorbent kitchen paper. With the point of a knife, lift out the inner ring on each round to form a hollow case. Put the cases on a baking sheet and place in the oven for a few minutes to crisp the insides. Cool completely.

Make the filling by mashing the sardines thoroughly and mixing them with the yogurt and tomato puree. Add salt and pepper to taste and stir in the lemon juice and Parmesan. Spoon into the prepared cases and garnish with watercress.

MAKES EIGHT TO TEN

VARIATIONS

- Canned skippers (smoked sprats), tuna or salmon may be used instead of sardines. Reduce the quantity of tomato purée to 5 ml / 1 tsp to balance the lighter flavour of these fish.

GRAVAD LAX

2 pieces unskinned salmon fillet, total weight about 1 kg / 2¼ lb, scaled
200 g / 7 oz salt
90 g / 3½ oz caster sugar
50 g / 2 oz white peppercorns, crushed
90 g / 3½ oz fresh dill, plus extra to garnish

MUSTARD SAUCE

30 ml / 2 tbsp Swedish mustard (or other mild mustard)
10 ml / 2 tsp caster sugar
15 ml / 1 tbsp chopped fresh dill
45–60 ml / 3–4 tbsp sunflower oil
lemon juice to taste
salt and pepper

Score the skin on each salmon fillet in 4 places. Mix the salt, sugar and peppercorns in a bowl.

Sprinkle a third of the salt mixture on the base of a shallow dish. Place one salmon fillet, skin side down, on the mixture. Cover with a further third of the salt mixture and add half the dill. Arrange the second fillet, skin side up, on top. Cover with the remaining salt mixture and dill.

Cover with foil. Place a plate or oblong baking sheet or tin on top of the fish and weight it down. Leave in the refrigerator for 36 hours, during which time the salt mixture will become a brine solution. Turn the whole fillet 'sandwich' every day and baste with the liquor.

For the sauce, mix the mustard, sugar and dill. Add the oil very slowly, beating all the time to make a thick sauce. Stir in a little lemon juice with salt and pepper to taste.

Drain off the brine, scrape away the dill and peppercorns before serving. Serve thinly sliced, garnished with fresh dill, with the mustard sauce.

SERVES FOUR TO SIX

SCALLOPED COD'S ROE

butter for greasing
400 g / 14 oz smoked cod's roe, skinned
salt
white wine vinegar
45 ml / 3 tbsp single cream
browned breadcrumbs
4 clean scallop shells
(ask your fishmonger in advance)

SAUCE
25 g / 1 oz butter
25 g / 1 oz plain flour
300 ml / ½ pint milk
salt and pepper
15 ml / 1 tbsp chopped parsley

Make the sauce. Melt the butter in a saucepan. Stir in the flour and cook over a low heat for 2–3 minutes, without allowing the mixture to colour. Gradually add the milk, stirring constantly until the sauce boils and thickens. Add salt and pepper to taste and stir in the parsley. Cover the surface of the sauce with damp greaseproof paper and set aside.

Grease 4 scallop shells. Set the oven at 200°C / 400°F / gas 6. Put the cod's roe in a saucepan with water to cover. Flavour the water with a little salt and vinegar and bring to simmering point. Poach the cod's roe for 10 minutes, remove with a slotted spoon and set aside on a plate until tepid; the roe will firm up.

Chop the cod's roe and add it to the parsley sauce with the cream. Mix lightly. Divide the cod's roe mixture between the prepared scallop shells, top with the browned breadcrumbs and place on a baking sheet. Bake for 2–3 minutes or until the sauce bubbles and the browned breadcrumbs are crisp.

SERVES FOUR

CRAB AU GRATIN

25 g / 1 oz butter
25 g / 1 oz plain flour
300 ml / ½ pint milk
salt and pepper
400 g / 14 oz white crab meat, flaked
100 g / 4 oz Gruyère cheese, grated
50 g / 2 oz fresh white breadcrumbs
30 ml / 2 tbsp grated Parmesan cheese

GARNISH
tomato slices
parsley sprigs

Melt the butter in a saucepan. Stir in the flour and cook over low heat for 2–3 minutes, without allowing the mixture to colour. Gradually add the milk, stirring constantly until the sauce boils and thickens. Season with salt and pepper to taste.

Stir the crab meat and Gruyère into the sauce. Spoon into individual ramekins, sprinkle with the breadcrumbs and Parmesan cheese and brown under a moderate grill for 2-3 minutes. Garnish with tomato slices and parsley sprigs and serve at once.

SERVES SIX

MRS BEETON'S TIP

The crab meat mixture may be served in crab shells, if liked. Make sure the shells are scrupulously clean and dry. Give them an attractive gloss by buffing them with a piece of absorbent kitchen paper dipped in oil.

PEPERONATA

A lively starter from Italy, peperonata is perfect for serving with prosciutto or salami.

45 ml / 3 tbsp olive oil
1 large onion, sliced
2 garlic cloves, crushed
350 g / 12 oz tomatoes, peeled, seeded and cut in quarters
2 large red peppers, seeded and cut in thin strips
1 large green pepper, seeded and cut in thin strips
1 large yellow pepper, seeded and cut in thin strips
2.5 ml / ½ tsp coriander seeds, lightly crushed (optional)
salt and pepper
15 ml / 1 tbsp red wine vinegar (optional)

Heat the oil in a large frying pan, add the onion and garlic and fry over gentle heat for 10 minutes. Add the tomatoes, peppers and coriander seeds, if used, with salt and pepper to taste. Cover and cook gently for 1 hour, stirring from time to time. Add more salt and pepper before serving if necessary. To sharpen the flavour, stir in the red wine vinegar, if liked.

SERVES FOUR

ASPARAGUS WITH HOT BUTTER SAUCE

36 (6 each) or 48 (8 each) asparagus spears, trimmed
175 g / 6 oz butter
white pepper
lemon juice

Cook the asparagus in simmering water in a tall narrow saucepan or on a rack over boiling water in a roasting tin for about 10 minutes, until tender.

Meanwhile, melt the butter. Add pepper and lemon juice to taste and pour over the drained asparagus.

SERVES SIX

VARIATIONS

- **Asparagus Hollandaise** Cook as above. Serve hot, with Hollandaise Sauce (page 190).
- **Asparagus Polonaise** Cook as above. Melt 45 ml / 3 tbsp butter in a frying pan, add 60 g / 2 oz fresh white breadcrumbs and cook until golden. Stir in the chopped yolks of 4 hard-boiled eggs, with 30 ml / 2 tbsp chopped parsley. Spoon over the asparagus.

EGGS BENEDICT

A delicious dish for brunch.

Hollandaise Sauce (page 190)
2 English muffins, split
30 ml / 2 tbsp butter
4 slices of ham
4 eggs

Make the Hollandaise Sauce following the method given on page 190.

Toast the muffins or bread slices, then butter them. Trim the ham slices to fit the bread. Put the trimmings on the hot muffins or toast and cover with the ham slices. Put on a large heated platter or individual plates and keep hot.

Poach the eggs and drain them well. Put an egg on each piece of ham, cover with about 15 ml / 1 tbsp of the Hollandaise sauce and serve the remaining sauce separately.

SERVES FOUR

HUMMUS

Serve as a starter or snack, with crudités,
French bread, hot pitta or crispbreads.

150 g / 5 oz chick peas
2 garlic cloves, very finely chopped or crushed
salt
90 ml / 6 tbsp olive oil
60 ml / 4 tbsp tahini (bought, or see page 137)
60 ml / 4 tbsp lemon juice
chopped parsley, extra virgin olive oil
and / or paprika to garnish

Soak and cook the chick peas, following the method given for Felafel, page 137. Drain thoroughly, then mash and sieve or crush in a mortar with a pestle to a smooth paste. An alternative, and much easier method, is to process the chick peas in a blender or food processor.

Add the garlic and salt to taste. Stir briskly until well mixed, then gradually work in the olive oil, as when making Mayonnaise (see page 197). The chick peas should form a creamy paste. Work in the tahini slowly, adding it a teaspoonful at a time at first. When the mixture is creamy work in lemon juice to taste. Transfer to a shallow serving bowl and sprinkle with your chosen garnishes.

SERVES SIX TO EIGHT

SPICY NUTS

2 tbsp salted butter
1 tbsp Worcestershire sauce
¼ tsp cumin
1 garlic clove, crushed with 1 tsp salt
¼ tsp cayenne pepper
350 g / 12 oz unsalted nuts of your choice
salt to taste

Preheat oven to 160°C / 325°F / gas 3. Melt the butter in a frying pan, over a gentle heat. Add all the ingredients except the nuts and stir for 2–3 minutes.

Add the nuts and stir until evenly coated. Spread on a baking sheet and bake for 15 to 20 minutes, shaking occasionally.

Sprinkle with salt to taste and serve immediately. Alternatively, allow to cool, store in an airtight container and serve gently reheated in a warm oven or over a moderate heat in a lightly-oiled frying pan.

BLOODY MARY

Makes a classic aperitif.

1 part vodka
2 parts tomato juice
Worcestershire sauce
lemon juice
Tabasco
salt and pepper
ice to serve

Mix the vodka and tomato juice. Add a few drops of hot Tabasco and other ingredients to taste. Pour over crushed ice or ice cubes to serve.

GARNISHES

The following classic garnishes should be added just before the food is served so that they look really fresh. Prepare the garnishing ingredients in advance. Keep them covered (if necessary, chilled), ready to add at the last minute.

HERBS

Fresh herb sprigs add colour and interest. They should also provide the diner with a clue as to the dominant flavour of the dish. Wash and dry sprigs well and use them in moderation. Parsley is a popular garnish but can be an irritating extra when it is unrelated to the ingredients it supposedly enhances. Other herbs used for garnishing include coriander, dill, basil, chervil, fennel and borage.

SALAD LEAVES

Watercress or mustard and cress are typical garnishes. These must be perfectly fresh and crisp. Shredded lettuce, rocket, celery leaves and other salad leaves all make attractive garnishes with the right foods. They complement grilled and fried foods, boiled hams, quiches and pies, but do not go with sauced dishes.

If the salad garnish is intended to be eaten, spoon a little French-type dressing over it just before serving. If you do not want to add an oil and vinegar dressing, trickle a few drops of walnut or hazelnut oil and a little fresh lemon juice over.

SALAD VEGETABLES

Tomatoes, cucumber, radishes and other vegetables that are generally eaten raw in salad contribute colour and texture when used as a garnish for hot and cold dishes.

Tomato Roses Use a small, sharp-pointed knife to thinly pare a strip of peel and flesh from the outside of a ripe tomato. Cut around the fruit in a spiral, then arrange the strip of peel in a neat rosette to represent a rose.

Radish Roses Make small 'V' cuts all around the base of a radish, then carefully pare off the vegetable from the point of the 'V' downwards, leaving each piece attached at the base in the form of a petal. Work more rows of cuts around the radish, from the base up towards the top. Then place the radish in a bowl of iced water and leave to stand for at least 30 minutes, or longer. The rose will gradually open.

Spring Onion Curls Trim a spring onion, then make slits down the green part to shred the onion, leaving the fine pieces attached at the white end. Place in a bowl of iced water for at least 30 minutes. The shreds will curl. This curling technique may also be used for celery, by shredding a length of celery stick, leaving the pieces attached at the end of the stick.

VEGETABLES

Cooked or raw vegetable garnishes introduce colour and flavour as well as texture. Neatly cut carrot, turnip, swede or leek are all examples of vegetables that make excellent garnishes for hot sauced dishes. Blanch them briefly to accentuate colour and flavour, softening their texture slightly.

Mushrooms are also classic garnishes. Toss them in hot oil or butter, add some chopped herbs if appropriate, then arrange them neatly with sauced, or grilled foods.

Julienne Cut thin slices of vegetable, then cut fine sticks, each about 2.5–5 cm / 1–2 inches long. Depending on the vegetable, the julienne may be blanched before use. A combination of vegetables, such as carrot and leek, make an attractive garnish.

Vegetable Flowers or Shapes Prepared, sliced vegetables should be parboiled until tender before being cut in decorative shapes. Use aspic cutters to stamp flowers or shapes out of the vegetables. Carrots, turnips, potatoes and swedes are all suitable. Shapes may also be stamped out of salad vegetables, such as cucumber or large white radishes; these should not be cooked.

Carrot Flowers Use a small, pointed knife to carve the outside of a carrot into petals. Simple but highly effective flowers may be made by simply cutting fine 'V' strips lengthways out of the carrot, then slicing the carrot thinly and blanching the slices in boiling water.

Turned Mushrooms Use small, perfect button mushrooms. Using a small pointed knife, cut off thin, narrow strips of peel from the centre of the mushroom outwards to the edge of the cap. Shape the cuts in spirals.

FRUIT

Citrus fruits are commonly used with fish, poultry and meat dishes. Slices or wedges are the simplest garnishes; twists, strips of pared rind and fruit cups are also used.

Most other fresh fruits are suitable for garnishing but they should always echo the main ingredients in terms of flavour. Any fruit which is liable to discolour should be cut just before use, dipped in lemon juice, then drained.

Lemon Twists Use this technique for lemon, lime or small orange slices. Cut thin slices of fruit (not so thin that they flop). Make a cut from the centre of the slice outwards, then twist the fruit.

Pared Citrus Rind Pare the rind thinly from the fruit, then cut it into fine strips. Simmer the strips in water until tender, then drain well. Use with fish, meat or vegetables as well as with sweet dishes.

Salads

Crisp and refreshing or full-flavoured and satisfying, salads play many roles in the modern menu. Try classics such as Salad Niçoise and Waldorf Salad, or adventurous combinations such as Fennel and Cucumber Salad.

RULES OF SUCCESSFUL SALADS

- Ingredients both raw and cooked must be fresh and in prime condition.
- Select ingredients which complement each other in flavour and texture.
- Do not use so many ingredients that the salad ends up as a kaleidoscope of unrecognizable, clashing flavours.
- Ingredients such as apple and cut beetroot, which discolour or shed colour, should be prepared and added just before serving.
- Salads leaves and greens which become limp quickly should be dressed at the last minute.
- The salad dressing should moisten, blend and develop the flavour of the main ingredients. It should not dominate the dish.

SIDE SALADS

Side salads should be simple, with clearly defined flavours and a light dressing that complement the main dish.

Green Salad Do not underestimate the value of a good, crisp, really fresh lettuce lightly tossed with a well-seasoned, oil-based dressing. This makes an ideal accompaniment for grilled fish, meat or poultry, or may be served with the cheese course. A classic green salad accentuates the richness of the main dish and refreshes the palate.

Mixed Green Salad This should consist of green ingredients, for example salad leaves, cucumber, finely sliced green pepper, celery, spring onions, watercress, mustard and cress, and avocado. A mixed green salad is ideal for serving with foods such as a quiche, with baked potatoes (topped with low-fat soft cheese, butter, soured cream or fromage frais) and with cold roast meats or grilled pork sausages.

Mixed Salad This type of side salad usually consists of a base of leaves, with other green ingredients, topped with raw items, such as tomatoes, radishes, grated carrots, shredded cabbage, beetroot and red or yellow peppers. A mixed salad goes well with cold meats and poultry, cheese or eggs.

Satisfying Side Salads Pasta, rice, beans, grains and potatoes all make good salads, and do not have to be mixed with a cornucopia of ingredients. They should be perfectly cooked, then tossed with selected herbs, such as parsley, mint, basil or tarragon. Additional ingredients should be kept to the minimum. In keeping with the main dish, mayonnaise, yogurt, fromage frais, soured cream or an oil-based mixture may be used to dress the salad.

MAIN COURSE SALADS

Fish and seafood, poultry, meat, game and dairy produce all make excellent salads. Beans and pulses are also suitable. The main food should feature in the same way as for a hot dish, with supporting ingredients and a full-flavoured dressing. It should stand out clearly as the star of the salad, without competition from other ingredients. The salad may be served on a base of shredded lettuce and a garnish of herbs, nuts or croûtons of fried bread may be included to balance the texture where necessary. Main course salads often have very plain accompaniments – chunks of crusty bread or a baked potato are usually all that is required.

SALAD NIÇOISE

salt and pepper
225 g / 8 oz French beans, topped and tailed
2 hard-boiled eggs, cut in quarters
3 small, best quality tomatoes, cut in quarters
1 x 198 g / 7 oz can tuna, drained and flaked
50 g / 2 oz good quality, natural black olives
1 large lettuce, separated into leaves
1 x 50 g / 2 oz can anchovy fillets, drained, to garnish

DRESSING
45 ml / 3 tbsp olive oil or a mixture of olive and sunflower oil
1 garlic clove, crushed
salt and pepper
pinch of English mustard powder
pinch of caster sugar
15 ml / 1 tbsp wine vinegar

Bring a small saucepan of salted water to the boil. Add the beans and cook for 5 minutes or until just tender. Drain, refresh under cold water and drain once more.

Make the dressing by mixing all the ingredients in a screw-topped jar. Close the jar tightly; shake vigorously until well blended.

Put the beans into a large bowl with the eggs, tomatoes, garlic, tuna and most of the olives. Pour over the dressing and toss lightly. Season with salt and pepper to taste.

Line a large salad bowl with the lettuce leaves. Pile the tuna mixture into the centre and garnish with the remaining olives and the anchovy fillets. Serve immediately.

SERVES FOUR TO SIX

FRENCH BEAN AND TOMATO SALAD

salt and pepper
225 g / 8 oz French beans, trimmed
3 tomatoes, peeled, seeded and quartered
15 ml / 1 tsp snipped chives

DRESSING

45 ml / 3 tbsp walnut or sunflower oil
10 ml / 2 tsp white wine vinegar
5 ml / 1 tsp lemon juice
pinch of caster sugar
pinch of mustard powder
1 garlic clove, crushed

Make the dressing by mixing all the ingredients in a screw-topped jar. Add salt and pepper to taste, close the jar tightly and shake vigorously until well blended.

Bring a small saucepan of salted water to the boil. Add the beans and cook for 5–10 minutes or until just tender. Drain, rinse briefly under cold water, drain again, then tip into a bowl. Immediately add the dressing and toss the beans in it. Leave to cool.

Add the tomatoes and toss lightly. Taste the salad and add more salt and pepper if required. Turn into a salad bowl, sprinkle with the chives and serve.

SERVES FOUR

MICROWAVE TIP

Wash the beans. Drain lightly, leaving some moisture on the pods. Place them in a roasting bag, tie the top loosely with an elastic band and microwave on High for 5 minutes. Shake the bag carefully, set it aside for 1 minute, then transfer the contents to a bowl and add the dressing and remaining ingredients.

COLESLAW

Coleslaw looks marvellous in a natural cabbage bowl. Use a sharp knife to cut out the centre of a Savoy cabbage, using the cut portion for the coleslaw. Rinse the cabbage bowl under cold water, shake off excess moisture and dry between the leaves with absorbent kitchen paper. Trim the base of the cabbage bowl so that it stands neatly.

450 g / 1 lb firm white or Savoy cabbage, finely shredded
100 g / 4 oz carrots, coarsely grated
2 celery sticks, thinly sliced (optional)
150 ml / ¼ pint Mayonnaise (page 197) or plain yogurt
salt and pepper
fresh lemon juice (see method)

Mix all the ingredients in a salad bowl, adding enough lemon juice to give the mayonnaise or yogurt a tangy taste. Chill before serving.

SERVES FOUR

VARIATION

- **Fruit and Nut Slaw** Core and dice, but do not peel, 1 red-skinned eating apple. Toss in 15 ml / 1 tbsp lemon juice, then add to the slaw with 25 g / 1 oz seedless raisins or sultanas and 25 g / 1 oz chopped walnuts, almonds or hazelnuts.

CABBAGE CRUNCH

100 g / 4 oz white cabbage, shredded
225 g / 8 oz red cabbage, shredded
4 celery sticks, chopped
2 carrots, cut into matchsticks
1 green pepper, seeded and thinly sliced
4 ready-to-eat dried apricots, thinly sliced
100 g / 4 oz pecan nuts or walnuts, chopped
50 g / 2 oz sunflower seeds

DRESSING

1 hard-boiled egg yolk
salt and pepper
1.25 ml / ¼ tsp prepared mustard
dash of Worcestershire sauce
pinch of caster sugar
10 ml / 2 tsp cider vinegar
15 ml / 1 tbsp sunflower oil
30 ml / 2 tbsp double cream

Make the dressing. Sieve the egg yolk into a bowl. Gradually work in the salt and pepper, mustard, Worcestershire sauce, caster sugar and vinegar. Add the oil gradually, beating constantly. Whip the cream in a clean bowl, then fold it into the dressing. Mix all the salad ingredients together and toss in the dressing.

SERVES SIX

MRS BEETON'S TIP

Full-flavoured, firm-textured salads like Coleslaw and Cabbage Crunch make excellent accompaniments to piping-hot baked potatoes. Not only does the flavour of the salad complement the potatoes but the textures also marry well.

TOMATO SALAD

Sun-warmed tomatoes, freshly picked, are perfect for this salad. In the classic Italian version, olive oil is the only dressing, but a little red wine vinegar may be added, if preferred.

450 g / 1 lb best quality tomatoes, peeled and sliced
salt and pepper
pinch of caster sugar (optional)
45 ml / 3 tbsp extra-virgin olive oil
5 ml / 1 tsp chopped fresh basil
fresh basil sprigs to garnish

Put the tomatoes in a serving dish and sprinkle lightly with salt and pepper. Add the sugar, if used. Pour over the olive oil and sprinkle with chopped basil. Garnish with basil sprigs.

SERVES FOUR TO SIX

VARIATIONS

- **Mozzarella and Tomato Salad** Interleave the sliced tomatoes with sliced mozzarella cheese. Cover and leave to marinate for at least an hour before serving.
- **Tomato and Onion Salad** A popular salad to serve with cold meats. Omit the basil. Very thinly slice 1 red or white onion and separate the slices into rings. Sprinkle these over the tomatoes. Sprinkle with sugar, salt and pepper, and a few drops of cider vinegar as well as the oil.
- **Minted Tomato Salad with Chives** Omit the basil. Sprinkle 15 ml / 1 tbsp chopped fresh mint and 45 ml / 3 tbsp snipped chives over the tomatoes before adding the oil. Garnish with sprigs of mint.

CUCUMBER IN YOGURT

1 large cucumber
salt and pepper
300 ml / ½ pint plain or Greek strained yogurt, chilled
15 ml / 1 tsp vinegar (optional)
30 ml / 2 tbsp chopped mint
pinch of sugar

Cut the cucumber into small dice and place it in a colander. Sprinkle with salt, leave for 3–4 hours, then rinse and drain thoroughly. Pat the cucumber dry on absorbent kitchen paper.

Stir the yogurt, vinegar (if used), mint and sugar together in a bowl. Add the cucumber and mix well. Taste and add salt and pepper if required.

SERVES FOUR TO SIX

VARIATION

- **Tzatziki** The combination of cucumber and yogurt is an internationally popular one. This is a Greek-style variation. Grate the cucumber instead of dicing it. Omit the vinegar. The mint is optional but a crushed garlic clove and 15 ml / 1 tbsp finely chopped onion are essential. Mix all the ingredients and serve with warm, fresh bread for a refreshing first course.

MRS BEETON'S TIP

Serve within 1 hour of making, or the liquid in the cucumber may thin the yogurt and spoil the consistency of the salad.

FENNEL AND CUCUMBER SALAD

1 large cucumber, diced
6 radishes, sliced
1 fennel bulb, sliced
1 garlic clove, crushed
5 ml / 1 tsp chopped mint
2 eggs, hard-boiled and quartered, to garnish

DRESSING
30 ml / 2 tbsp olive oil
15 ml / 1 tbsp lemon juice
salt and pepper

Combine the cucumber, radishes, fennel and garlic in a salad bowl. Sprinkle with the mint. Make the dressing by shaking all the ingredients in a tightly-closed screw-topped jar. Pour over the salad, toss lightly and serve with the hard-boiled egg garnish.

SERVES SIX

GRAPEFRUIT AND CHICORY SALAD

3 grapefruit
3 small heads of chicory
50 g / 2 oz seedless raisins
15 ml / 1 tbsp grapefruit juice
45 ml / 3 tbsp sunflower oil
2.5 ml / ½ tsp French mustard
salt and pepper
mustard and cress to garnish

Cut the grapefruit in half. Cut the fruit into segments and put them into a bowl. Remove all the pulp and pith from the grapefruit shells; stand the shells upside down on absorbent kitchen paper to drain.

Shred the chicory, reserving some neat rounds for the garnish, and add to the grapefruit segments with all the remaining ingredients except the garnish. Toss the mixture lightly together, then pile back into the grapefruit shells. Garnish with the cress and reserved chicory and serve at once.

SERVES SIX

WALDORF SALAD

4 sharp red dessert apples
2 celery sticks, thinly sliced
25 g / 1 oz chopped or broken walnuts
75 ml / 5 tbsp Mayonnaise (page 197)
30 ml / 2 tbsp lemon juice
pinch of salt
lettuce leaves (optional)

Core the apples, but do not peel them. Cut them into dice. Put them in a bowl with the celery and walnuts. Mix the mayonnaise with the lemon juice. Add salt to taste and fold into the apple mixture. Chill. Serve on a bed of lettuce leaves, if liked.

SERVES FOUR

VARIATION

- **Waldorf Salad with Chicken** Make as above, but use only 2 apples. Add 350 g / 12 oz diced cold cooked chicken. For extra flavour and colour, add 50 g / 2 oz small seedless green grapes.

ORANGE AND ORTANIQUE SALAD

3 oranges, peeled and sliced
3 ortaniques, peeled and sliced (see Mrs Beeton's Tip)
1 mild Italian or Spanish onion, cut in rings
12 black olives
30 ml / 2 tbsp chopped mint to garnish

DRESSING

75 ml / 5 tbsp olive oil
30 ml / 2 tbsp orange juice
15 ml / 1 tbsp red wine vinegar
5 ml / 1 tsp soy sauce
5 ml / 1 tsp liquid honey
salt and pepper

Make the dressing by mixing all the ingredients in a screw-topped jar. Close the jar tightly and shake vigorously until well blended.

Put the dressing in a large bowl and add the orange, ortanique and onion slices. Cover the bowl and set aside for 1–2 hours.

When ready to serve, arrange the fruit and onion slices on a large platter, add the olives and drizzle the remaining dressing over the top. Sprinkle with the mint.

SERVES SIX

MRS BEETON'S TIP

The ortanique – a cross between an orange and a tangerine – was developed in Jamaica. The fruit is easy to peel and segment, and is very sweet and juicy. If unavailable, substitute tangerines, grapefruit or limes.

BEAN SPROUT SALAD

225 g / 8 oz bean sprouts
1 small orange, peeled and sliced
100 g / 4 oz Chinese leaves, shredded
2 celery sticks, thinly sliced
salt and pepper

DRESSING

45 ml / 3 tbsp olive oil or a mixture of olive and sunflower oil
15 ml / 1 tbsp white wine vinegar
1 garlic clove, crushed
2.5 ml / ½ tsp soy sauce
pinch of caster sugar

Pick over the bean sprouts, wash them well, then dry thoroughly. Cut the orange slices into quarters.

Make the dressing by mixing all the ingredients in a screw-topped jar. Close the jar tightly and shake vigorously. Combine the bean sprouts, Chinese leaves, celery and orange in a bowl. Pour over the dressing and toss lightly. Season to taste and serve at once.

SERVES FOUR

MRS BEETON'S TIP

Bean sprouts are highly nutritious. To grow your own, place dried soya beans, mung beans or alfalfa seeds in a clean glass jar. The jar should be no more than one-sixth full. Cover the jar with a piece of muslin held in place by an elastic band. Fill the jar with cold water, then drain off the liquid. Store in a cool dark place. Rinse the beans in fresh water every day. They should start to sprout in 2–3 days and will be ready to eat in 5–6 days.

PEAR, NUT AND DATE SALAD

1 small crisp lettuce, separated into leaves
3 ripe dessert pears
15 ml / 1 tbsp lemon juice
100 g / 4 oz stoned dates
50 g / 2 oz walnuts
10 ml / 2 tsp chopped parsley
45 ml / 3 tbsp French Dressing (page 46)

Wash the lettuce leaves and dry them thoroughly. Reserve 6 outer leaves, shred the rest and put them in a bowl. Peel and halve the pears, put them in a second bowl and add the lemon juice. Toss lightly to preserve the colour.

Add the dates, walnuts and parsley to the shredded lettuce, pour over the dressing and toss lightly. Arrange the outer lettuce leaves on six individual plates. Put a pear half on each plate, cut side up. Pile the date mixture into the centre of each fruit, cover and chill for 1 hour before serving.

SERVES SIX

PEPPER SALAD

2 large green peppers
2 large red peppers
2 large yellow peppers
1 mild Italian or Spanish onion, thinly sliced in rings
100 ml / 3½ fl oz olive oil
salt and pepper (optional)

Wash the peppers and pat dry with absorbent kitchen paper. Grill under moderate heat, turning the peppers frequently with tongs until the skins blister, then char all over. Immediately transfer the peppers to a large bowl and cover with several layers of absorbent kitchen paper.

Alternatively, put the grilled peppers in a polythene bag. When cold, rub off the skin under cold water. Remove cores and seeds and cut or tear the peppers into thin strips.

Put the pepper strips on a serving platter, arrange the onion rings around the rim, and drizzle the olive oil over the top. Add salt and pepper to taste, if liked. Serve at once.

SERVES SIX TO EIGHT

RICE SALAD

200 g / 7 oz long-grain rice
salt
60 ml / 4 tbsp olive oil
30 ml / 2 tbsp white wine vinegar
2 spring onions, finely chopped
1 carrot, finely diced and blanched
1 small green pepper, seeded and finely diced
3 gherkins or 8 cornichons, finely diced
30 ml / 2 tbsp snipped chives
watercress to serve

Place the rice in a saucepan. Pour in 450 ml / ¾ pint cold water. Add a little salt, then bring to the boil. Cover the pan tightly and reduce the heat to the lowest setting. Leave the rice for 15 minutes, turn off the heat and leave for a further 15 minutes without removing the lid. The rice should have absorbed all the liquid. Drain if necessary.

Stir in the oil and vinegar while the rice is still hot. Add the vegetables and chives; mix well. Pile on a dish and garnish with watercress. Serve at once.

SERVES FOUR TO SIX

RICE AND ARTICHOKE SALAD

*Basmati rice gives this salad the best flavour.
Make the vinaigrette at least 1 hour before use,
to allow the flavours to develop.*

200 g / 7 oz long-grain rice
salt
100 ml / 3½ fl oz French Dressing (see Mrs Beeton's Tip)
1 garlic clove, crushed
1 x 397 g / 14 oz can artichoke hearts, drained and halved
30 ml / 2 tbsp snipped chives to garnish

Place the rice in a saucepan and pour in 450 ml / ¾ pint cold water. Cover the pan tightly and reduce the heat to the lowest setting. Leave the rice for 15 minutes, turn off the heat and leave for a further 15 minutes without lifting the lid.

Mix the dressing and garlic, add to the hot rice and fork it in lightly. Leave until cool.

Just before serving, fork the artichoke hearts into the rice. Sprinkle with the chives as garnish.

SERVES FOUR

MRS BEETON'S TIP

To make French dressing, mix together a pinch of mustard powder, a pinch of caster sugar and salt and pepper to taste in a small bowl. Add 30 ml / 2 tbsp wine vinegar and whisk until the sugar has dissolved. Whisk in 90 ml / 6 tbsp olive oil (or a mixture of olive and sunflower oil) and check the dressing for salt and pepper before using.

CAESAR SALAD

As the egg in this salad is only lightly cooked,
it is crucial that it be perfectly fresh,
and purchased from a reputable source.

3 garlic cloves, peeled but left whole
2 cos lettuces, separated into leaves
150 ml / ¼ pint olive oil
4 large, thick slices of bread, crusts removed, bread cubed
1 egg
juice of 1 lemon
1 x 50 g / 2 oz can anchovy fillets, drained
50 g / 2 oz Parmesan cheese, grated
salt and pepper

Cut 1 garlic clove in half and rub it all around the inside of a salad bowl. Wash the lettuce leaves and dry them thoroughly. Tear into small pieces and put in the salad bowl.

Heat 60 ml / 4 tbsp of the olive oil in a small frying pan, add the remaining garlic cloves and fry over gentle heat for 1 minute. Add the bread cubes and fry until golden on all sides. Remove from the pan with a slotted spoon and drain on absorbent kitchen paper. Discard the garlic and oil in the pan.

Add the remaining olive oil to the lettuce and toss until every leaf is coated. Bring a small saucepan of water to the boil, add the egg and cook for 1 minute. Using a slotted spoon remove it from the water and break it over the lettuce. Add the lemon juice, anchovies, cheese, salt and pepper and toss lightly.

Add the croûtons of fried bread and toss again. Serve as soon as possible, while the croûtons are still crisp.

SERVES SIX

POTATO SALAD

salt and pepper
6 large new potatoes or waxy old potatoes
150 ml / ¼ pint Mayonnaise (page 197)
3 spring onions, chopped
30 ml / 2 tbsp chopped parsley

Bring a saucepan of salted water to the boil, add the potatoes in their jackets and cook for 20–30 minutes until tender. Drain thoroughly.

When cool enough to handle, peel and dice the potatoes. Put them in a bowl and add the Mayonnaise while still warm. Lightly stir in the spring onions and parsley, with salt and pepper to taste. Cover, leave to become quite cold and stir before serving.

SERVES SIX

VARIATIONS

- **French Potato Salad** Substitute 100 ml / 3½ fl oz French Dressing (see Mrs Beeton's Tip, page 46) for the mayonnaise. Omit the spring onions, increase the parsley to 45 ml / 3 tbsp and add 5 ml / 1 tsp chopped fresh mint and 5 ml / 1 tsp snipped chives.
- **German Potato Salad** Omit the mayonnaise and spring onions. Reduce the parsley to 5 ml / 1 tsp and add 5 ml / 1 tsp finely chopped onion. Heat 60 ml / 4 tbsp vegetable stock in a saucepan. Beat in 15 ml / 1 tbsp white wine vinegar and 30 ml / 2 tbsp oil. Add salt and pepper to taste. Pour over the diced potatoes while still hot and toss lightly together. Serve at once, or leave to become quite cold.
- **Potato Salad with Apple and Celery** Follow the basic recipe above, but add 2 sliced celery sticks and 1 diced red-skinned apple tossed in a little lemon juice.

MRS BEETON'S POTATO SALAD

This should be made two or three hours before it is to be served so that the flavours have time to mature. Cold beef, turkey or other poultry may be thinly sliced or cut into chunks and combined with the potato salad to make a light main course dish.

10 small cold cooked potatoes
60 ml / 4 tbsp tarragon vinegar
90 ml / 6 tbsp salad oil
salt and pepper
15 ml / 1 tbsp chopped parsley

Cut the potatoes into 1-cm / ½-inch thick slices. For the dressing, mix the tarragon vinegar, oil and plenty of salt and pepper in a screw-topped jar. Close the jar tightly and shake vigorously until well blended.

Layer the potatoes in a salad bowl, sprinkling with a little dressing and the parsley. Pour over any remaining dressing, cover and set aside to marinate before serving.

SERVES SIX

VARIATIONS

- **Potato and Anchovy Salad** Drain a 50 g / 2 oz can of anchovy fillets, reserving the oil. Chop the fillets. Use the oil to make the dressing. Sprinkle the chopped anchovies between the layers of potato with the dressing.
- **Potato and Olive Salad** Thinly slice 50 g / 2 oz stoned black olives. Chop 2 spring onions, if liked, and mix them with the olives. Sprinkle the olives between the potato layers.
- **Potato Salad with Pickles** Dice 1 pickled gherkin and 1–2 pickled onions. Reduce the vinegar to 15–30 ml / 1–2 tbsp when making the dressing. Sprinkle the pickles between the layers of potato with the dressing.

LENTIL AND ONION SALAD

225 g / 8 oz brown or green lentils, soaked for 2–3 hours in water to cover
1 salt-free vegetable or onion stock cube
1 red onion, thinly sliced in rings
30 ml / 2 tbsp finely chopped parsley

DRESSING

45 ml / 3 tbsp light olive oil
salt and pepper
pinch of mustard powder
pinch of caster sugar
5 ml / 1 tsp soy sauce
15 ml / 1 tbsp red wine vinegar

Put the lentils in a saucepan with cold water to cover. Bring to the boil, add the crumbled stock cube, lower the heat and simmer for 30–40 minutes until tender but not mushy.

Meanwhile make the dressing by mixing all the ingredients in a screw-topped jar. Close the jar tightly and shake vigorously until well blended.

Drain the cooked lentils thoroughly, tip into a serving bowl and immediately add the dressing. Toss lightly, then add the onion rings with half the parsley. Allow the salad to stand for at least 1 hour before serving to allow the flavours to blend. Sprinkle with the remaining parsley.

SERVES FOUR TO SIX

MRS BEETON'S TIP

Italian red onions are at their best in late spring. Mild, sweet and crisp, they are ideal for stuffing, roasting whole or in salads.

TABBOULEH

This delicious salad is served all over the middle East.
Its central ingredient is bulgur or cracked wheat,
which has been hulled and parboiled.
It therefore needs little or no cooking.

125 g / 4½ oz bulgur wheat
2 tomatoes, peeled, seeded and diced
1 small red onion, finely chopped
2 spring onions, finely chopped
100 g / 4 oz fresh parsley, very finely chopped
50 g / 2 oz fresh mint, very finely chopped
juice of 1 lemon
30 ml / 2 tbsp olive oil
salt and pepper
crisp lettuce leaves to serve

Put the bulgur wheat in a large bowl, add water to generously cover and set aside for 45–60 minutes. Line a sieve or colander with a clean tea-towel and strain the bulgur. When most of the liquid has dripped through, scoop the bulgur up in the tea-towel and squeeze it strongly to extract as much of the remaining liquid as possible. Tip the bulgur into a bowl.

Add the tomatoes, onion, spring onions, parsley, mint, lemon juice and oil, with salt and pepper to taste. Mix well.

Dome the tabbouleh in the centre of a large platter. Arrange the lettuce leaves around the rim to be used as scoops.

SERVES SIX TO EIGHT

VARIATION

- **Tabbouleh in Peppers or Tomatoes** Serve tabbouleh in halved, boiled and well-drained pepper shells or in scooped-out tomato shells.

FLAGEOLET BEAN SALAD

The fresh green colour and tender flavour of flageolets makes them an ideal candidate for a light summer salad. Add a little crumbled, grilled bacon or drained, flaked tuna and serve with French bread for a simple summer lunch.

225 g / 8 oz dried flageolet beans, soaked overnight in water to cover
1 bouquet garni
150 ml / ¼ pint Mayonnaise (page 197)
1 onion, finely chopped
15 ml / 1 tbsp finely chopped parsley
salt

Drain the beans, put them in a clean saucepan with the bouquet garni and add fresh water to cover. Bring the water to the boil, boil briskly for 10 minutes, then lower the heat and simmer the beans for 1¼–1½ hours until tender.

Drain the beans thoroughly, remove the bouquet garni and tip into a bowl. While the beans are still warm, stir in the Mayonnaise, onion and parsley, with salt to taste. Toss lightly.

Allow the salad to stand for at least 3 hours before serving to allow the flavours to blend.

SERVES FOUR TO SIX

MRS BEETON'S TIP

Do not add salt to the water when cooking pulses such as dried flageolet beans as it toughens them. Pulses are delicious when cooked in vegetable stock, but take care to use a salt-free variety.

CHICKEN AND CELERY SALAD

1 large lettuce, separated into leaves
1 celery heart
350 g / 12 oz cooked chicken, cut into small pieces
10 ml / 2 tsp tarragon or white wine vinegar
salt and pepper
150 ml / ¼ pint Mayonnaise (page 197)

GARNISH
lettuce leaves
2 hard-boiled eggs, sliced or chopped
stoned black olives and/or gherkin strips

Wash the lettuce leaves and dry them thoroughly. Shred the outer leaves with the celery. Put in a bowl with the chicken and vinegar. Toss lightly and add salt and pepper to taste.

Spoon the chicken mixture into a bowl or on to a platter. Coat with the Mayonnaise. Garnish with lettuce leaves, sliced or chopped egg and olives and/or gherkin strips.

SERVES SIX

VARIATION

- If preferred, keep the lettuce heart as a base for the chicken and celery mixture. For a substantial, meal-in-one salad, toss in some cooked pasta shapes or cooked rice.

SPINACH AND BACON SALAD

450 g / 1 lb fresh young spinach
150 g / 5 oz button mushrooms, thinly sliced
1 small onion, thinly sliced
15 ml / 1 tbsp oil
6 rindless streaky bacon rashers, cut into strips
75 ml / 5 tbsp French Dressing (page 46)

Remove the stalks from the spinach, wash the leaves well in cold water, then dry thoroughly on absorbent kitchen paper. If time permits, put the leaves in a polythene bag and chill for 1 hour.

Tear the spinach into large pieces and put into a salad bowl with the mushrooms and onion.

Heat the oil in a small frying pan and fry the bacon until crisp. Meanwhile toss the salad vegetables with the French Dressing. Pour in the hot bacon and fat, toss lightly to mix and serve at once.

SERVES FOUR

MRS BEETON'S TIP

If preferred, the bacon may be grilled until crisp and crumbled into the salad just before serving.

Fish & Seafood

Versatile, quick and relatively light, main courses based on fish and seafood are ideal dinner party choices.

FILLET OF SOLE BONNE FEMME

butter for greasing
16 lemon sole fillets
275 g / 10 oz mushrooms
50 g / 2 oz butter
12 black peppercorns
2–3 parsley stalks
25 g / 1 oz plain flour
300 ml / ½ pint Fish Stock (page 186)
salt and pepper
lemon juice
2 shallots, slices
15 ml / 1 tbsp chopped parsley
250 ml / 8 fl oz dry white wine

Grease a shallow ovenproof baking dish and a piece of foil large enough to cover it. Arrange the sole fillets on the base. Set the oven at 180°C / 350°F / gas 4. Cut off the mushroom stems and set them aside. Slice the mushroom caps and scatter them over the fish.

Melt 25 g / 1 oz of the butter in a saucepan, add the mushroom stems, peppercorns and parsley stalks. Cook over gentle heat for 10 minutes. Add the flour and cook over a low heat for 2–3 minutes, without allowing the mixture to colour. Gradually add the stock and simmer, stirring for 3–4 minutes. Rub the sauce through a sieve into a clean pan. Add salt, pepper and lemon juice to taste. Cover the surface with damp greaseproof paper and set aside.

Sprinkle the shallots and parsley over the fish, sprinkle with salt and pepper and pour in the wine. Cover with the foil and bake for 20 minutes.

Using slotted spoon and fish slice, transfer the fish to a warmed serving dish and keep hot. Strain the cooking liquid into a saucepan. Boil it rapidly until reduced by half.

Meanwhile return the sauce to a gentle heat and bring to simmering point. Stir the sauce into the reduced cooking liquid with the remaining butter. As soon as the butter has melted, pour the sauce over the fish. Place under a hot grill until lightly browned. Serve at once.

SERVES EIGHT

SOLE MEUNIÈRE

50 g / 2 oz plain flour
salt and pepper
4 large sole fillets
75 g / 3 oz butter
30 ml / 2 tbsp chopped parsley
juice of 1 lemon
lemon wedges to garnish

Mix the flour with salt and pepper and spread out in a shallow bowl. Lightly coat the fish fillets in the seasoned flour.

Melt the butter in a frying pan and fry the fillets over moderate heat for about 7 minutes, turning once, until golden brown.

Using a slotted spoon and a fish slice, carefully transfer the fish to a warmed serving dish and keep hot. Continue heating the butter until it is nut brown. Add the parsley.

Pour the butter over the fish, sprinkle with lemon juice and serve at once, garnished with lemon wedges.

SERVES FOUR

PLAICE MORNAY

butter for greasing
350 ml / 12 fl oz milk
1 onion, finely chopped
1 carrot, finely chopped
1 celery stick, finely chopped
1 bouquet garni
salt and pepper
8 plaice fillets
25 g / 1 oz butter
25 g / 1 oz plain flour
100 g / 4 oz Gruyère cheese, grated
50 g / 2 oz Parmesan cheese, grated
1.25 ml / ¼ tsp mustard powder
fresh chervil sprigs to garnish

Grease a shallow flameproof dish. Combine the milk, vegetables and bouquet garni in a saucepan. Add salt and pepper to taste. Bring to the boil, lower the heat and simmer for 10 minutes. Set aside to cool.

Fold the plaice fillets in three, skin side inwards. Strain the flavoured milk into a deep frying pan and heat to simmering point. Add the fish and poach for 6–8 minutes or until the fish is cooked. Using a slotted spoon, transfer the fish to the prepared dish. Cover with buttered greaseproof paper and keep warm. Reserve the cooking liquid in a jug.

Melt the butter in a saucepan, add the flour and cook for 1 minute, stirring continously. Gradually add the reserved cooking liquid, whisking constantly until the sauce thickens.

Mix the cheeses and stir half the mixture into the sauce, with the mustard. Remove the buttered paper from the fish, pour the sauce over the top and sprinkle with the remaining cheese mixture. Brown briefly under a hot grill. Garnish and serve.

SERVES FOUR

BAKED MULLET

25 g / 1 oz butter
225 g / 8 oz onions, thinly sliced
225 g / 8 oz tomatoes, peeled, seeded and sliced
4 x 225 g / 8 oz grey mullet, cleaned and trimmed
100 ml / 3½ fl oz dry white wine
salt and pepper
15 ml / 1 tbsp chopped fresh tarragon or
5 ml / 1 tsp dried tarragon
1 lemon, sliced
sippets or croûtons (see Mrs Beeton's Tip), to garnish

Use the butter to grease a shallow ovenproof baking dish and a sheet of greaseproof paper. Set the oven at 190°C / 375°F / gas 5.

Spread out the onion rings on the base of the dish and top with the sliced tomatoes. Lay the fish on top of the vegetables and pour the wine over. Sprinkle with salt, pepper and tarragon.

Arrange the lemon slices on top of the fish and cover loosely with the buttered greaseproof paper. Bake for 30 minutes. Garnish with sippets or croûtons and serve from the dish.

SERVES FOUR

MRS BEETON'S TIP

To make sippets, toast white or granary bread until golden. Cut into small triangles, cubes or fancy shapes. For croûtons, fry small shapes of stale bread in sunflower oil until golden and crisp.

RED MULLET BAKED IN FOIL

6 red mullet, cleaned and trimmed
50 g / 2 oz butter
salt and pepper
juice of ½ lemon

GARNISH
lemon wedges
parsley sprigs

Set the oven at 190°C / 375°F / gas 5. Lay each mullet on a piece of foil large enough to enclose it completely. Dot with butter, sprinkle with salt and pepper and add a little lemon juice. Fasten the packages by folding the edges of the foil firmly together over the fish.

Put the packages on a baking sheet and bake for 20–30 minutes. Remove the fish from the foil, reserving the cooking juices. Transfer to a warm platter, pour over the cooking juices and serve at once, garnished with lemon and parsley.

SERVES SIX

BAKED MURRAY COD

oil for greasing
4 portions of cod fillet, total weight about 450 g / 1 lb, skinned
2 rindless fat back bacon rashers, chopped
1 large onion, finely chopped
250–350 ml / 8–12 fl oz milk
1 bay leaf
salt and pepper
25 g / 1 oz dried white breadcrumbs

Grease an ovenproof baking dish just large enough to hold all the fish in a single layer. Set the oven at 230°C / 450°F / gas 8. Cook the bacon and onion together in a heavy-bottomed pan until the fat runs from the bacon and the onion is slightly softened. Spread the mixture out in the dish. Top with the fish.

Pour the milk into a saucepan, add the bay leaf and bring to the boil. Remove the bay leaf, add salt and pepper to taste and pour the hot milk into the dish to the depth of the fish. The tops of the fish fillets should be exposed.

Cover the fish thickly with the breadcrumbs. Bake for 20 minutes or until the fish is tender and the topping browned. Serve piping hot with peas or spinach.

SERVES FOUR

BAKED FRESH SARDINES

butter for greasing
45 ml / 3 tbsp olive oil
2 large onions, finely chopped
45 ml / 3 tbsp medium-dry white wine
225 g / 8 oz tomatoes, peeled, seeded and chopped
salt and pepper
900 g / 2 lb sardines, cleaned and trimmed
50 g / 2 oz fresh white breadcrumbs
25 g / 1 oz butter
watercress sprigs to garnish

Grease a shallow ovenproof baking dish. Set the oven at 180° / 350°F / gas 4. Heat the oil in a small saucepan, add the onions and fry gently for about 5 minutes until lightly browned. Add the wine and boil until the volume is reduced by two thirds. Stir in the tomatoes, with salt and pepper to taste. Cook for 3–4 minutes.

Pour the tomato mixture into the prepared dish, arrange the sardines on top and sprinkle with the breadcrumbs. Dot with the butter and bake for 25 minutes. Serve hot, garnished with watercress.

SERVES SIX

HERRINGS WITH MUSTARD SAUCE

4 herrings
10 ml / 2 tsp lemon juice
salt and pepper
10 ml / 2 tsp mustard powder
2 egg yolks
50 g / 2 oz butter
30 ml / 2 tbsp double cream
15 ml / 1 tbsp chopped capers
15 ml / 1 tbsp chopped gherkin

Scale the herrings, cut off the heads and remove the bones. Sprinkle the flesh with the lemon juice and plenty of salt and pepper. Grill under moderate heat for 3–5 minutes on each side. Transfer to a warmed serving dish and keep hot.

Combine the mustard and egg yolks in the top of a double saucepan, place over hot water and whisk until creamy. Add the butter, a small piece at a time, whisking well after each addition.

When the sauce thickens, remove the pan from the heat and stir in the cream, capers and gherkin. Add salt and pepper to taste, pour into a sauceboat and serve with the fish.

SERVES FOUR

MACKEREL NIÇOISE

4 small mackerel
25 g / 1 oz butter
30 ml / 2 tbsp olive oil
1 large onion, finely chopped
1 garlic clove, crushed
125 ml / 4 fl oz medium-dry white wine
10 ml / 2 tsp tomato purée
pinch of powdered saffron
salt and pepper
225 g / 8 oz tomatoes, peeled, seeded and chopped

GARNISH
parsley sprigs
stoned black olives
lemon slices

Rinse the fish inside and out and pat dry on absorbent kitchen paper. Melt the butter in the oil in a large frying pan. Add the onion and garlic and fry for 3–4 minutes until soft but not coloured. Place the fish on top.

Mix the wine and tomato purée together and pour over the fish. Add the saffron, salt and pepper. Bring the liquid to simmering point and poach the fish for 10 minutes.

Using a slotted spoon and a fish slice, carefully transfer the fish to a warmed serving dish and keep hot. Add the chopped tomatoes to the cooking liquid and boil briskly for 5 minutes, stirring occasionally.

Pour the sauce over the fish, garnish with parsley, olives and lemon slices and serve at once.

SERVES FOUR

MACKEREL WITH GOOSEBERRY SAUCE

Gooseberry sauce is such a classic accompaniment to mackerel that in France the fruit is known as groseille à maquereau.

50 g / 2 oz plain flour
salt and pepper
8 mackerel fillets
50 g / 2 oz butter
juice of 1 lemon
45 ml / 3 tbsp chopped parsley

SAUCE

450 g / 1 lb gooseberries, topped and tailed
45 ml / 3 tbsp dry still cider
25 g / 1 oz butter
15 ml / 1 tbsp caster sugar

Make the sauce by combining the gooseberries, cider and butter in a small saucepan. Bring the liquid to simmering point and poach the fruit, stirring occasionally, until soft. Purée the mixture by passing it through a sieve set over a small pan. Stir in the sugar.

Spread out the flour in a shallow bowl, add salt and pepper, and coat the fish lightly all over. Melt the butter in a large frying pan, add the fish and fry gently for 5–7 minutes or until browned, turning once. Using a slotted spoon and a fish slice, transfer the fish to a warmed serving dish and keep hot.

MICROWAVE TIP

The gooseberries can be cooked in the microwave. Combine the cider and butter in a mixing bowl and heat for 1 minute on High. Add the fruit, stir, cover the bowl and cook for 5–7 minutes or until soft. Stir once or twice during cooking.

Heat the gooseberry sauce. Continue to heat the butter in the frying pan until it becomes light brown. Stir in the lemon juice and parsley and pour over the fish. Pour the gooseberry sauce into a jug or sauceboat and serve at once with the fish.

SERVES FOUR

TWEED KETTLE

575 g / 1¼ lb middle cut salmon
500 g / 17 fl oz Fish Stock (page 186)
250 ml / 8 fl oz dry white wine
pinch of ground mace
salt and pepper
25 g / 1 oz chopped shallots or snipped chives
5 ml / 1 tsp chopped parsley
25 g / 1 oz butter
30 ml / 2 tbsp plain flour

Put the salmon in a saucepan with the fish stock, wine and mace. Add salt and pepper to taste. Bring the liquid to simmering point and simmer gently for 10–15 minutes or until the fish is just cooked through.

Using a slotted spoon and a fish slice, transfer the fish to a large plate. Remove the skin and bones and return them to the stock in the pan. Transfer the skinned fish to a warmed serving dish and keep hot. Simmer the stock and fish trimmings for 10 minutes, then strain into a clean pan. Simmer gently, uncovered, until reduced by half. Stir in the shallots or chives and the parsley and remove from the heat.

In a small bowl, blend the butter with the flour. Gradually add small pieces of the mixture to the stock, whisking thoroughly after each addition. Return to the heat and simmer for 5 minutes, stirring. Pour over the fish and serve at once.

SERVES FOUR

BAKED SALMON

800 g / 1¾ lb middle cut salmon
salt and pepper
grated nutmeg
2 small shallots, chopped
15 ml / 1 tbsp chopped parsley
25 g / 1 oz butter
100 ml / 3½ fl oz dry white wine

Set the oven at 190°C / 375°F / gas 5. Wash and dry the fish and lay it on a sheet of heavy-duty foil large enough to enclose it completely. Lift the edges of the foil and pinch the corners together to make a shallow case. Sprinkle the fish with salt, pepper and a little grated nutmeg. Add the chopped shallots and sprinkle the parsley over the fish. Dot with the butter and pour over the wine.

Carefully lift the edges of the foil and pinch them together to enclose the fish and the wine. Carefully transfer the foil parcel to an ovenproof dish. Cook for 25 minutes.

Drain the fish and serve hot with Hollandaise Sauce (page 190) or leave to cool in the cooking juices, drain and serve with green salad, thinly sliced cucumber arranged like scales and Mayonnaise (page 197).

SERVES SIX TO EIGHT

MRS BEETON'S TIP

To make pastry fleurons, roll out 215 g / 7½ oz puff pastry on a floured board. Cut into rounds, using a 5-cm / 2-inch cutter. Move the cutter halfway across each round and cut in half again, making a half moon and an almond shape. Arrange the half moons on a baking sheet, brush with beaten egg and bake in a preheated oven at 200°C / 400°F / gas 6 for 8–10 minutes. The almond shapes may be either baked as biscuits or re-rolled and cut to make more fleurons.

ANGEVIN SALMON TROUT

butter for greasing
1 x 1 kg / 2¼ lb salmon trout
1 onion, finely chopped
375 ml / 13 fl oz rosé wine
15 g / ½ oz butter
15 ml / 1 tbsp plain flour
30 ml / 2 tbsp double cream
salt and pepper
125 ml / 4 fl oz Hollandaise Sauce (page 190)

GARNISH
Fleurons (see Mrs Beeton's Tip, page 66)
watercress sprigs

Generously butter a fairly deep ovenproof dish large enough to hold the whole fish. Set the oven at 160°C / 325°F / gas 3.

Cut the fins from the fish and thoroughly wash the body cavity. Put the fish in the dish, curling it round if necessary. Add the onion. Mix the wine with 100 ml /3½ fl oz water and pour over the fish. Oven-poach for 30 minutes.

Using a slotted spoon and a fish slice, carefully transfer the fish to a wooden board. Remove the skin and keep the fish hot. Strain the cooking liquid into a saucepan and boil until reduced by one third.

Melt the butter in a clean saucepan, add the flour and cook for 1 minute, stirring constantly. Gradually add the reduced cooking liquid, stirring all the time until the mixture comes to the boil. Remove from the heat and add the cream, with salt and pepper to taste. Beat in the hollandaise sauce.

Fillet the fish, placing the fillets on a warmed serving dish. Coat with half the sauce, pouring the rest into a sauceboat. Garnish with the pastry fleurons and the watercress and serve the fish at once, with the remaining sauce.

SERVES FOUR

SALMON TROUT WITH AVOCADO SAUCE

1 x 1.8–2 kg / 4–4½ lb salmon trout
Court Bouillon (page 186)

SAUCE
2 avocados
30 ml / 2 tbsp lime or lemon juice
45 ml / 3 tbsp oil
salt and pepper

Clean the salmon trout, if necessary, but leave the head and tail on.

Place the fish in a kettle or suitable pan and pour in the court bouillon to cover the fish by at least 3.5 cm / 1¼ inches. Top up the water if necessary. Bring the liquid to a bare simmer, cover the pan tightly and cook for about 30 minutes or until the thickest part of the fish yields slightly when pressed.

Carefully transfer the fish to a board or platter. Skin as much of the fish as possible. Turn the fish on to a serving platter, or carefully turn it over, and strip off the remaining skin. Cover loosely with a cloth and set aside to cool.

Make the sauce by mashing the avocado flesh in a bowl with the remaining ingredients until it has the consistency of thick mayonnaise. A food processor or blender may be used, but take care not to over-process the mixture.

When the fish is cold, use a little of the sauce to mask it. Serve the remaining sauce separately.

SERVES SIX TO EIGHT

MONKFISH AND BACON KEBABS

125 ml / 4 fl oz olive oil
1 garlic clove, crushed
5 ml / 1 tsp lemon juice
5 ml / 1 tsp dried oregano
800 g / 1¾ lb monkfish, cleaned, trimmed and cut into 2-cm / ¾-inch cubes
225 g / 8 oz rindless streaky bacon rashers
200 g / 7 oz small mushrooms
salt and pepper

Combine the olive oil, garlic, lemon juice and oregano in a shallow bowl large enough to hold all the monkfish cubes in a single layer. Mix well, add the fish, and marinate for 15 minutes. Drain the monkfish, reserving the marinade.

Thread a piece of bacon on to a kebab skewer. Add a cube of fish, then a mushroom, weaving the bacon between them. Continue to add the fish and mushrooms, each time interweaving the bacon, until the skewer is full. Add a second rasher of bacon if necessary. Fill five more skewers in the same way. Sprinkle with salt and pepper.

Grill the monkfish kebabs under moderate heat for 10–15 minutes, basting frequently with the reserved marinade.

SERVES SIX

HADDOCK AND FENNEL FLAMBÉ

dried fennel stalks (see method)
225 g / 8 oz butter
60 ml / 4 tbsp brandy
1 kg / 2¼ lb haddock or hake fillets
salt and pepper
15 ml / 1 tbsp chopped fresh fennel
lemon wedges to garnish

Have ready a metal serving dish large enough to accommodate the rack of your grill pan. Pile dried fennel stalks on the dish to a depth of 5 cm / 2 inches. Melt 200 g / 7 oz of the butter in a small saucepan. Keep it warm over a candle burner at the table. Have the brandy ready in a small jug. You will also need an all-metal soup ladle and a long match or taper.

Place the fish, skin side up, on the rack of the grill pan. Grill under moderate heat for 5 minutes, then carefully remove the skin. Turn the fillets over carefully, using a fish slice. Sprinkle with salt, pepper and chopped fennel, and dot with the remaining butter. Grill for a further 10 minutes.

Place the rack containing the cooked fish over the fennel and carry it to the table. Pour the brandy into the soup ladle and warm it over the candle burner. Pour the warm brandy over the fish, then light the brandy and dried fennel.

When the flames have died down, transfer the fish to individual plates. Garnish with the lemon wedges. Serve with the melted butter.

SERVES FOUR

VARIATIONS

- **Mackerel Flambé** Slash the sides of 4 mackerel and tuck a few fennel leaves inside each. Season the fish, grill for 10–12 minutes, then flambé as suggested above.

FRENCH FRIED HADDOCK

1 kg / 2¼ lb haddock fillets, skinned
250 ml / 8 fl oz milk
100 g / 4 oz plain flour
salt and pepper
oil for deep frying
lemon wedges, to serve

Cut the fish into 4–5 portions. Pour the milk into a shallow bowl. Spread out the flour in a second bowl; add salt and pepper. Dip the pieces of fish first into milk and then into flour, shaking off the excess.

Put the oil for frying into a deep wide pan. Heat the oil to 180–190°C / 350–375°F or until a cube of bread added to the oil browns in 30 seconds.

If using a deep-fat fryer, follow the manufacturer's instructions.

Carefully lower the fish into the hot oil and fry for 3–5 minutes until evenly browned. Drain on absorbent kitchen paper and serve on a warmed platter, with lemon wedges.

SERVES FOUR TO FIVE

MRS BEETON'S TIP

The fish should be of uniform thickness for frying. Any thin pieces, such as tail ends, should be folded double before flouring the fish.

KEDGEREE

No Victorian country-house breakfast would have been complete without kedgeree. Hard-boiled egg and parsley are the traditional garnish, sometimes arranged in the shape of the cross of St Andrew.

salt and pepper
150 g / 5 oz long-grain rice
125 ml / 4 fl oz milk
450 g / 1 lb smoked haddock
50 g / 2 oz butter
15 ml / 1 tbsp curry powder
2 hard-boiled eggs, roughly chopped
cayenne pepper to taste

GARNISH
15 g / ½ oz butter
1 hard-boiled egg, white and yolk sieved separately
15 ml / 1 tbsp chopped parsley

Bring a saucepan of salted water to the boil. Add the rice and cook for 12 minutes. Drain thoroughly, rinse under cold water and drain again. Place the strainer over a saucepan of simmering water to keep the rice warm.

Put the milk in a large shallow saucepan or frying pan with 125 ml / 4 fl oz water. Bring to simmering point, add the fish and poach gently for 4 minutes. Using a slotted spoon and a fish slice, transfer the haddock to a wooden board. Discard the cooking liquid.

Remove the skin and any bones from the haddock and break up the flesh into fairly large flakes. Melt half the butter in a large saucepan. Blend in the curry powder and add the flaked fish. Warm the mixture through. Remove from the heat, lightly stir in the chopped eggs; add salt, pepper and cayenne.

Melt the remaining butter in a second pan, add the rice and toss until well coated. Add salt, pepper and cayenne. Add the rice to the haddock mixture and mix well. Pile the kedgeree on to a warmed dish.

Dot the kedgeree with the butter, garnish with sieved hard-boiled egg yolk, egg white and parsley and serve at once.

SERVES FOUR

PRAWN CURRY

15 ml / 1 tbsp ground coriander
2.5 ml / ½ tsp ground cumin
2.5 ml / ½ tsp chilli powder
2.5 ml / ½ tsp turmeric
1 garlic clove, crushed
250 ml / 8 fl oz Fish Stock (page 186)
30 ml / 2 tbsp oil
1 large onion, finely chopped
45 ml / 3 tbsp tomato purée
2 tomatoes, peeled, seeded and chopped
450 g / 1 lb peeled cooked prawns
juice of 1 lemon
10 ml / 2 tsp coconut cream (optional)
fresh coriander sprigs, to garnish

Mix all the spices in a small bowl. Add the garlic and mix to a paste with a little of the stock. Set aside.

Heat the oil in a frying pan, add the onion and fry for 4–5 minutes until golden brown. Add the tomato purée and spice mixture, then cook for 1–2 minutes. Stir in the remaining stock and tomatoes, cover the pan and simmer gently for 20 minutes.

Add the prawns and lemon juice to the pan, with the coconut cream, if used. Stir until the coconut cream dissolves, then simmer for 5 minutes more. Garnish with fresh coriander sprigs and serve with Basmati rice.

SERVES FOUR

KOULIBIAC

Koulibiac is a large oblong pastry from Russia filled with a mixture of cooked rice and salmon. Smoked salmon offcuts or canned salmon may be used instead of fresh salmon. Instead of following the method described below, cook the fish on a covered plate which fits tightly over the saucepan, if preferred. This is good either hot or cold and is therefore ideal for formal meals, buffets or picnics.

butter for greasing
450 g / 1 lb salmon fillet or steaks
salt and pepper
juice of ½ lemon
175 g / 6 oz long-grain rice
50 g / 2 oz butter
1 onion, chopped
60 ml / 4 tbsp chopped parsley
4 hard-boiled eggs, roughly chopped
15 ml / 1 tbsp chopped fresh tarragon (optional)
450g / 1 lb puff pastry
1 egg, beaten, to glaze
150 ml / ¼ pint soured cream to serve

Lay the salmon on a piece of greased foil large enough to enclose it completely. Sprinkle with salt, pepper and a little of the lemon juice, then wrap the foil around the fish, sealing the edges.

Place the rice in a large saucepan and add 450 ml / ¾ pint water. Bring to the boil, lower the heat and cover the pan. Simmer the rice for 10 minutes, then place the foil-wrapped fish on top of the rice. Cover the pan again and cook for about 10 minutes more or until the grains of rice are tender and all the water has been absorbed.

At the end of the cooking time, remove the foil-packed salmon from the pan. Transfer the fish to a board, reserving all the cooking juices, then discard the skin and any bones. Coarsely flake the flesh and set the fish aside. Tip the cooked rice into a bowl.

Melt half the butter in a small saucepan. Add the onion and cook over low heat for about 15 minutes until it is soft but not browned. Mix the cooked onion with the rice and add the salmon and parsley, with salt and pepper to taste. Put the chopped hard-boiled eggs in a bowl. Stir in the remaining lemon juice and add the tarragon, if used. Melt the remaining butter and trickle it over the eggs.

Set the oven at 220°C / 425°F / gas 7. Cut a large sheet of foil, at least 30 cm / 12 inches long. On a floured board, roll out the pastry to a rectangle measuring about 50 x 25 cm / 20 x 10 inches. Trim the pastry to 43 x 2 5 cm / 17 x 10 inches. Cut the trimmings into long narrow strips. Set aside.

Lay the pastry on the foil. Spoon half the rice mixture lengthways down the middle of the pastry. Top with the egg mixture in an even layer, then mound the remaining mixture over the top. Fold one long side of pastry over the filling and brush the edge with beaten egg. Fold the other side over and press the long edges together firmly. Brush the inside of the pastry at the ends with egg and seal them firmly.

Use the foil to turn the koulibiac over so that the pastry seam is underneath, then lift it on to a baking sheet or roasting tin. Brush all over with beaten egg and arrange the reserved strips of pastry in a lattice pattern over the top. Brush these with egg too.

Bake the koulibiac for 30–40 minutes, until the pastry is well puffed and golden. Check after 25 minutes and if the pastry looks well browned, tent a piece of foil over the top to prevent it from overcooking.

Serve in thick slices with a small dish of soured cream.

SERVES EIGHT

CRAB-STUFFED CANNELLONI

butter for greasing
12 cannelloni
salt and pepper
225 g / 8 oz crab meat
50 g / 2 oz fresh white breadcrumbs
3 spring onions, chopped
225 g / 8 oz ricotta cheese
600 ml / 1 pint Fresh Tomato Sauce (page 193)
225 g / 8 oz mozzarella cheese, sliced

Grease a large, shallow baking dish with butter. Alternatively, prepare 4 individual gratin dishes. Cook the cannelloni in boiling salted water for 10–15 minutes. until tender. Drain and rinse in cold water, then lay out to dry on a clean tea-towel.

Set the oven at 190°C / 375°F / gas 5. Place the crab meat in a bowl and shred it with two forks. If using brown meat as well as white, add it after the white has been shredded. Mix in the breadcrumbs, spring onions and ricotta, with salt and pepper.

There are two ways of filling cannelloni: either put the crab mixture into a piping bag fitted with a large plain nozzle and force the mixture into the tubes, or use a teaspoon to fill the tubes. For those who are confident about using a piping bag the former method is less messy.

Lay the filled cannelloni in the prepared baking dish or dishes. Pour the tomato sauce over. Top with the mozzarella and bake for about 40 minutes, until golden brown.

SERVES FOUR

SPICY FISH SLICES

675 g / 1½ lb cod or hake fillets
7.5 ml / 1½ tsp salt
5 ml / 1 tsp turmeric
5 ml / 1 tsp chilli powder
90 ml / 6 tbsp oil
fresh coriander sprigs to garnish

Cut the fish into 2-cm / ¾-inch slices and spread them out in a shallow dish large enough to hold all the slices in a single layer. Mix the salt and spices in a bowl. Stir in enough water to make a thick paste. Rub the paste into the fish, cover and leave to marinate for 1 hour.

Heat the oil in a large frying pan. Add as much of the spiced fish as possible, but do not overfill the pan. Fry the fish for 5–10 minutes until golden brown all over, then remove from the pan with a slotted spoon. Drain on absorbent kitchen paper and keep hot while cooking the rest of the fish.

Garnish and serve hot, with rice or a small salad, if liked.

SERVES FOUR TO FIVE

SCAMPI JAMBALAYA

25 g / 1 oz butter
15 ml / 1 tbsp oil
2 onions, finely chopped
100 g / 4 oz cooked ham, diced
3 tomatoes, peeled and chopped
1 green pepper, seeded and finely chopped
1 garlic clove, crushed
pinch of dried thyme
salt and pepper
cayenne pepper
5 ml / 1 tsp Worcestershire sauce
225 g / 8 oz long-grain rice
125 ml / 4 fl oz hot Chicken Stock (page 187)
450 g / 1 lb peeled cooked scampi tails
100 g / 4 oz shelled cooked mussels (optional)
30 ml / 2 tbsp medium-dry sherry
fresh thyme sprigs to garnish

Melt the butter in the oil in a deep frying pan, add the onions and fry gently for 4–5 minutes until soft. Add the ham, tomatoes, green pepper and garlic, then stir in the thyme, with salt, pepper and cayenne to taste. Add the Worcestershire sauce and rice. Stir well. Add the hot stock, cover the pan and cook for 12 minutes.

Add the scampi to the pan, with the mussels, if used. Lower the heat, cover and simmer for 5 minutes more or until the rice is perfectly cooked. Stir in the sherry, garnish with thyme and serve at once.

SERVES FOUR

MRS BEETON'S TIP

Peeled cooked prawns may be substituted for the scampi. Large Mediterranean prawns are delicious in Jambalaya but ordinary prawns are quite suitable.

JAMAICAN FRIED FISH

225 g / 8 oz fish bones and trimmings
3 green peppers, seeded and sliced
3 onions, sliced
3 carrots, sliced
2 bay leaves, split in half
2 cm / ¾ inch fresh root ginger, peeled and finely chopped
8 peppercorns
1 blade of mace
salt
30 ml / 2 tbsp groundnut oil
90 ml / 6 tbsp malt vinegar
45 ml / 3 tbsp sunflower or corn oil
1 kg / 2¼ lb white fish fillets

Put the fish bones and trimmings in a large saucepan with the peppers, onions, carrots, bay leaves and ginger. Add the peppercorns and mace, with salt to taste. Pour in 350 ml / 12 fl oz water, bring to the boil and simmer uncovered for 35 minutes. Add the groundnut oil and vinegar and simmer for 2 minutes more. Strain the stock, reserving the vegetables as accompaniments for the fish, if liked. Keep hot.

Heat the sunflower or corn oil in a large frying pan, add the fish fillets and fry for 7–8 minutes, turning once, until just browned. Remove the fish from the oil with a slotted spoon and drain on absorbent kitchen paper.

Place the fish fillets in a warmed serving dish, pour the reserved stock over and serve at once, with the reserved vegetables.

SERVES SIX

VARIATION

- **Jamaican Fish Salad** Cook as suggested above, but allow the fish fillets to cool down in the stock. Chill. Garnish with olives and strips of pepper before serving.

SABO-NO-TERIYAKI

150 ml / ¼ pint soy sauce
45 ml / 3 tbsp mirin (see Mrs Beeton's Tip)
pinch of chilli powder
15 ml / 1 tbsp grated fresh root ginger
2 garlic cloves, crushed
4 mackerel, herring, salmon or bream fillets

Mix the soy sauce, mirin, chilli powder, ginger and garlic in a bowl. Stir well. Arrange the mackerel fillets in a shallow dish large enough to hold them all in a single layer. Pour the soy sauce mixture over, cover the dish and marinate for 2 hours.

Drain the fish, reserving the marinade. Cook under a hot grill for 5–10 minutes, brushing the fish several times with the reserved marinade during cooking. Serve at once.

SERVES FOUR

MRS BEETON'S TIP

If you cannot obtain mirin, which is sweet Japanese rice wine, use a mixture of 45 ml / 3 tbsp of dry sherry and 10 ml / 2 tsp sugar.

Meat & Poultry

Try a traditional recipe such as Roast Ribs of Beef with Yorkshire Pudding, an international favourite such as Goulash or a more formal dish such as Fillets of Duck with Rich Cherry Dressing.

ROAST CHICKEN WITH HONEY AND ALMONDS

1 x 1.5–1.8 kg / 3½–4 lb oven-ready roasting chicken
½ lemon
salt and pepper
45 ml / 3 tbsp honey
50 g / 2 oz flaked almonds
pinch of powdered saffron or 1 tsp fresh saffron strands
lightly toasted in a pan and crumbled
30 ml / 2 tbsp oil
watercress sprigs to garnish (optional)

Set the oven at 180°C / 350°F / gas 4. Rub the chicken all over with the cut lemon, then sprinkle with salt and pepper. Line a roasting tin with a piece of foil large enough to enclose the bird completely.

Put the bird into the foil-lined tin, then brush it all over with the honey. Sprinkle the nuts and saffron over, then trickle the oil very gently over the top. Bring up the foil carefully, tenting it over the bird so that it is completely covered. Make sure that the foil does not touch the skin. Seal the package by folding the edges of the foil over.

Roast for 1½–2 hours or until the chicken is cooked through. Open the foil for the last 10 minutes to allow the breast of the bird to brown. Transfer the chicken to a heated serving dish and garnish it with watercress if liked.

SERVES FOUR TO SIX

SPRING CHICKENS WITH PARSLEY

50 g / 2 oz parsley sprigs
100 g / 4 oz butter
salt and pepper
2 spring chickens weighing 900 g–1.4 kg / 2–3 lb each
300 ml / ½ pint double cream

GARNISH

1 lemon, cut in wedges
4 parsley sprigs

Strip the leaves from the parsley sprigs and chop them roughly. Soften half the butter in a bowl, beat well, then mix in half the parsley, with salt and pepper to taste. Place half the mixture in the body cavity of each bird.

Melt the remaining butter in a large frying pan, add the birds and brown them lightly all over. Add 150 ml / ¼ pint water, bring just to the boil, cover and cook gently for 40 minutes or until the birds are cooked through. Transfer the chickens to a plate and cut them in half. Arrange on a heated serving dish and keep hot.

Add the cream to the stock remaining in the pan and cook over low heat, stirring until the sauce is hot. Do not allow it to boil. Add the remaining parsley, taste the sauce, and add more salt and pepper if required. Pour the sauce over the chicken and garnish with lemon wedges and parsley sprigs.

SERVES FOUR

MRS BEETON'S TIP

If spring chickens are not available, substitute 1 x 1.4 kg / 3 lb roasting chicken. Stuff it with the parsley butter. Cook for about 1½ hours, adding extra water as necessary. When cooked, cut into quarters.

CHICKEN SUPREME

1 x 1.4–1.6 kg / 3–3½ lb chicken
1 litre / 1¾ pints Chicken (page 187) or Vegetable Stock (page 188)
chopped truffles or poached mushrooms, to garnish

SAUCE
50 g / 2 oz butter
4 button mushrooms, finely chopped
6 black peppercorns
4–5 parsley stalks
25 g / 1 oz plain flour
salt and pepper
lemon juice (see method)
150 ml / ¼ pint single cream
1 egg yolk
grated nutmeg

Truss the chicken neatly, put it into a large saucepan and pour over the stock. Bring the liquid to the boil, lower the heat, cover the pan and simmer for 1½–2 hours or until tender. After 1 hour, strain off 250 ml / 8 fl oz of the chicken stock. Blot the surface with a piece of absorbent kitchen paper to remove excess fat, then set the stock aside for use in the sauce.

Melt half the butter in a saucepan. Add the mushrooms, peppercorns and parsley stalks. Cook gently for 10 minutes, then stir in the flour. Cook over gentle heat for 2–3 minutes. Gradually add the reserved stock, stirring well to prevent the formation of lumps. Raise the heat and cook the sauce, stirring constantly, until it thickens. Rub through a sieve into a clean pan, add salt, pepper and lemon juice to taste and stir in half the cream. Cool the sauce slightly.

MRS BEETON'S TIP

The stock remaining in the pan when the chicken has been removed may be cooled, then chilled, so that the fat solidifies and can be removed easily. The skimmed stock may then be used for soup or in another recipe.

Beat the egg yolk and remaining cream with a little of the cooled sauce in a bowl. Add the contents of the bowl to the sauce and stir over gentle heat until heated. The yolk and cream enrich, rather than thicken the sauce. Do not boil or the yolk and cream will curdle. Whisk in the remaining butter, adding a knob at a time. Add nutmeg to taste.

Drain the cooked chicken, joint it into serving portions and transfer these to a heated serving dish. Pour the sauce over, garnish with truffles or mushrooms and serve.

SERVES FOUR TO SIX

DEVILLED CHICKEN

4 chicken breasts
30 ml / 2 tbsp oil
50 g / 2 oz butter, softened
15 ml / 1 tbsp tomato purée
2.5 ml / ½ tsp mustard powder
few drops of Tabasco sauce
10 ml / 2 tsp Worcestershire sauce
lemon or lime wedges to serve

Place the chicken breasts on a rack in a grill pan. Brush generously with oil and grill under moderate heat for 5 minutes on each side.

Meanwhile, prepare the devilled mixture. Beat the butter in a small bowl and gradually work in the tomato purée, mustard powder, Tabasco and Worcestershire sauce. Spread half the mixture over the chicken and grill for 5 minutes more, then turn the breasts over carefully, spread with the remaining mixture and grill for a further 5 minutes or until the chicken is thoroughly cooked. Transfer the chicken to plates or a serving dish and add lemon or lime wedges: the fruit juice may be squeezed over just before the chicken is eaten. Serve with baked jacket potatoes and a green salad.

SERVES FOUR

COQ AU VIN

The best coq au vin is made by marinating the chicken overnight in the red wine before cooking.

1 x 1.6 kg / 3½ lb chicken with giblets
1 bouquet garni
salt and pepper
75 g / 3 oz unsalted butter
15 ml / 1 tbsp oil
150 g / 5 oz belly of pickled pork or green (unsmoked) bacon rashers, rind removed and chopped
150 g / 5 oz button onions or shallots
30 ml / 2 tbsp brandy
175 g / 6 oz small button mushrooms
2 garlic cloves, crushed
575 ml / 19 fl oz burgundy or other red wine
15 ml / 1 tbsp tomato purée
25 g / 1 oz plain flour
croûtes of fried bread, to serve

Joint the chicken and skin the portions if liked. Place the giblets in a saucepan with 450 ml / ¾ pint water. Add the bouquet garni, salt and pepper. Cook gently for about 1 hour, then strain. Measure the stock and set aside 275 ml / 9 fl oz.

Set the oven at 150°C / 300°F / gas 2. Melt 40 g / 1½ oz of the butter in the oil in a flameproof casserole. Add the pork or bacon, with the onions. Cook over gentle heat for about 10 minutes until the onions are lightly coloured. Using a slotted spoon, transfer the bacon and onions to a plate.

Add the chicken portions to the fat remaining in the pan and brown lightly all over. Ignite the brandy (see Mrs Beeton's Tip). When the flames die down, pour it into the casserole. Add the reserved bacon and onions, with the mushrooms and garlic. Stir in the wine, giblet stock and tomato purée. Cover and cook in the oven for 1–1½ hours or until the chicken is cooked through and tender.

Using a slotted spoon, transfer the chicken portions to a heated serving dish. Arrange the bacon, mushrooms and onions over them. Cover with buttered greaseproof paper and keep hot. Return the casserole to the hob and simmer the liquid until reduced by about one-third.

Meanwhile make a beurre manié by blending the remaining butter with the flour in a small bowl. Gradually add small pieces of the mixture to the stock, whisking thoroughly after each addition. Continue to whisk the sauce until it thickens. Pour the sauce over the chicken. Garnish with croûtes of fried bread and serve.

SERVES FOUR TO SIX

MAKING CROÛTES

Cut rounds of baguette about 1 cm / ½ inch thick and fry in a tablespoon of sunflower oil with a knob of butter, until golden and crisp. Alternatively, butter both sides of the slices, place on a baking tray and bake in a preheated oven at 180°C / 350°F / gas 4 for 10 minutes, turning halfway, until crisp and golden.

MRS BEETON'S TIP

To flame the brandy, either pour it into a soup ladle and warm over low heat or warm it in a jug in the microwave for 15 seconds on High. Ignite the brandy (if warmed in a soup ladle it may well ignite spontaneously) and when the flames die down, pour it into the casserole.

LEMON CHICKEN

6 chicken breasts
salt and pepper
50 g / 2 oz butter
15 ml / 1 tbsp oil
1 onion, sliced
1 lemon, sliced
60 ml / 4 tbsp plain flour
250 ml / 8 fl oz Chicken Stock (page 187)
2–3 bay leaves
5 ml / 1 tsp caster sugar

Set the oven at 190°C / 375°F / gas 5. Season the chicken breasts with salt and pepper. Melt the butter and oil in a large frying pan, add the chicken and fry until golden brown all over. Using tongs or a slotted spoon, transfer to a casserole.

Add the onion and lemon slices to the fat remaining in the pan and fry over very gentle heat for about 15 minutes. Using a slotted spoon, transfer the onion and lemon to the casserole.

Sprinkle the flour into the fat remaining in the pan. Cook for 1 minute, then blend in the stock. Bring to the boil, stirring all the time. Add the bay leaves and sugar, with salt and pepper to taste. Pour over the chicken breasts in the casserole, cover and bake for about 45 minutes or until the chicken is tender. Remove the casserole lid 5 minutes before the end of the cooking time.

Remove the bay leaves before serving or reserve them as a garnish.

SERVES SIX

CHICKEN WINGS WITH GINGER

oil for greasing
12 chicken wings
juice of 1 lemon
2.5 ml / ½ tsp sesame oil
45 ml / 3 tbsp plain flour
10 ml / 2 tsp ground ginger
salt and pepper

SAUCE

60 ml / 4 tbsp preserved ginger in syrup, drained and chopped
30 ml / 2 tbsp medium-dry sherry
25 g / 1 oz butter

Remove and discard the ends from the chicken wings. Mix the lemon and oil together in a small bowl. Brush the mixture all over the chicken wings. Reserve the remaining lemon / oil mixture.

Spread out the flour in a shallow bowl and flavour with the ginger, salt and pepper. Add the chicken wings and turn them in the mixture until well coated.

Set the oven at 190°C / 375°F / gas 5. Spread out the chicken wings on a greased baking sheet and bake for 50–60 minutes, or until crisp and golden. Turn the wings occasionally during cooking.

Meanwhile, make the sauce. Add the ginger, sherry and butter to the remaining lemon / oil mixture, tip into a small saucepan and bring to the boil. Arrange the cooked chicken wings on a heated serving platter and pour the sauce over them. Serve with noodles or rice, if liked, and some stir-fried mixed vegetables.

SERVES FOUR

CHICKEN AND VEGETABLE STEW WITH COUSCOUS

50 g / 2 oz chick peas, soaked overnight in plenty of cold water
45 ml / 3 tbsp olive oil
8 chicken thighs, skinned if preferred
2 garlic cloves, crushed
1 large onion, chopped
1 green pepper, seeded and sliced
1 green chilli, seeded and chopped (optional)
15 ml / 1 tbsp ground coriander
5 ml / 1 tsp ground cumin
100 g / 4 oz carrots, sliced
100 g / 4 oz turnips, cut into chunks
450 g / 1 lb pumpkin, peeled, seeds removed and cut into chunks
450 g / 1 lb potatoes, cut into chunks
1 bay leaf
2 x 397 g / 14 oz cans chopped tomatoes
50 g / 2 oz raisins
150 ml / ¼ pint Chicken Stock (page 187) or water
salt and pepper
225 g / 8 oz courgettes, sliced
45 ml / 3 tbsp chopped parsley
350 g / 12 oz couscous
50 g / 2 oz butter, melted

Drain the chick peas, then cook them in plenty of fresh boiling water for 10 minutes. Lower the heat, cover the pan and simmer for 1½ hours, or until the chick peas are just tender. Drain.

Heat the oil in a very large flameproof casserole or saucepan. Add the chicken pieces and brown them all over, then, using a slotted spoon, remove them from the pan and set aside. Add the garlic, onion, pepper and chilli, if used, to the oil remaining in the pan and cook for 5 minutes, stirring.

Stir in the coriander and cumin, then add the carrots, turnips, pumpkin, potatoes, bay leaf, tomatoes, raisins and Chicken Stock or water. Season with salt and pepper to taste. Stir in the drained chick peas. Bring to the boil, then lower the heat and replace the chicken thighs, tucking them in among the vegetables. Cover and simmer gently for 1 hour. Stir in the courgettes and parsley, cover the pan and continue to cook gently for a further 30 minutes.

There are two options for preparing the couscous. The first is to line a steamer with scalded muslin, then sprinkle the couscous into it. Place the steamer over the simmering stew for the final 30 minutes' cooking, covering it tightly to keep all the steam in. Alternatively – and this is the easier method – place the couscous in a deep casserole or bowl and pour in fresh boiling water from the kettle to cover the grains by 2.5 cm / 1 inch. Cover and set aside for 15 minutes. The grains will absorb the boiling water and swell. If the couscous cools on standing, it may be reheated over a pan of boiling water or in a microwave for about 2 minutes on High.

To serve, transfer the couscous to a very large serving dish and pour over the hot melted butter. Fork up the grains and make a well in the middle. Ladle the chicken and vegetable stew into the well, spooning cooking juices over the couscous.

SERVES EIGHT

MRS BEETON'S TIP

Cubes of boneless lamb may be used instead of the chicken. The vegetables may be varied according to what is freshly available – marrow or green beans may be added or substituted for other ingredients. Couscous is usually accompanied by a hot, spicy condiment known as harissa. This paste, made from chillies, cumin, coriander, garlic, mint and oil, is deep red in colour and fiery of flavour. It is added to individual portions to taste but should be treated with respect.

TANDOORI CHICKEN

This dish is prepared a day in advance.

1 x 1.4–1.6 kg / 3–3½ lb chicken
15 ml / 1 tbsp cumin seeds
30 ml / 2 tbsp grated fresh root ginger
1 onion, grated
4 garlic cloves, crushed
5 ml / 1 tsp salt
5 ml / 1 tsp chilli powder
2.5 ml / 1 tsp turmeric
5 ml / 1 tsp garam masala (see Mrs Beeton's Tip, page 93)
few drops of red food colouring (optional)
juice of 2 lemons
150 ml / ¼ pint plain yogurt
30 ml / 2 tbsp oil

Skin the chicken. Keep it whole or cut it into 4 or 8 pieces. Toast the cumin seeds in a small ungreased frying pan over moderate heat for 1 minute. Grind them in a pepper mill, or use a pestle and mortar. Set the seeds aside.

Combine the ginger, onion, garlic, salt, chilli powder, turmeric and garam masala in a small bowl. Add the colouring, if used, then stir in the lemon juice and yogurt.

Prick the chicken with a fork and cut a few slits in the legs and breast. Rub the bird with the paste, pressing it deeply into the slits. Place in a shallow dish, cover tightly with foil and a lid and marinate for 12 hours or overnight.

Set the oven at 180°C / 350°F / gas 4. Put the chicken on a rack in a shallow roasting tin. Baste it with the oil and any remaining paste. Bake for 1½–2 hours, spooning over the oil and pan juices from time to time. When cooked, sprinkle with the toasted cumin seeds. Serve with Pilau Rice (see page 158) and a Tomato and Onion Salad (see page 138).

SERVES FOUR

MRS BEETON'S TIP

There are many versions of garam masala. The spice mix is usually dry, although some are mixed to a paste with water. They vary according to region and the cook's preference but the sweet spices are used to make the fragrant mixtures. Garam masala may be used in a wide variety of dishes, either added towards the end of the cooking time or combined with other spices in a paste. It may be sprinkled over the food during the final stages before serving. To make your own garam masala, toast 60 ml / 4 tbsp coriander seeds in a small ungreased frying pan, stirring all the time for a few minutes until they give off their aroma. Tip the seeds into a bowl and repeat the process with 30 ml / 2 tbsp cumin seeds, 15 ml / 1 tbsp black peppercorns, 10 ml / 2 tsp cardamom seeds, 3 cinnamon sticks and 5 ml / 1 tsp whole cloves, toasting each spice separately. When all the spices have been toasted and cooled, grind them to a powder in a coffee grinder (reserved for the purpose) or in a mortar with a pestle. Stir in 30 ml / 2 tbsp freshly grated nutmeg. Store in an airtight jar.

ENGLISH ROAST DUCK

fat for basting
Sage and Onion Stuffing (page 181)
1 x 1.8 kg / 4 lb oven-ready duck
salt and pepper
30 ml / 2 tbsp plain flour
300 ml / ½ pint duck stock or Chicken Stock (page 187)
(see Mrs Beeton's Tip)

Set the oven at 190°C / 375°F / gas 5. Spoon the stuffing into the duck and truss it. Weigh the duck and calculate the cooking time at 20 minutes per 450 g / 1 lb. Sprinkle the breast with salt. Put the duck on a wire rack in a roasting tin and prick the skin all over with a fork or skewer to release the fat. Roast for the required time, basting the duck occasionally with the pan juices and pouring away the excess fat as necessary. Test by piercing the thickest part of the thigh with the point of a sharp knife. The juices should run clear.

Transfer the duck to a heated platter, remove the trussing string and keep hot. Pour off most of the fat from the roasting tin, sprinkle in the flour and cook, stirring, for 2 minutes. Blend in the stock. Bring to the boil, then lower the heat and simmer, stirring, for 3–4 minutes. Add salt and pepper to taste. Serve in a gravyboat, with the duck.

SERVES FOUR

MRS BEETON'S TIP

If you have the duck giblets, use them as the basis of your stock. Put them in a saucepan with 1 sliced onion and 1 sliced carrot. Add 600 ml / 1 pint water. Simmer, covered, for 1 hour, then strain.

DUCK WITH ORANGE SAUCE

1 x 1.6–1.8 kg / 3½–4 lb oven-ready duck
salt and pepper
5 oranges
15 ml / 1 tbsp caster sugar
15 ml / 1 tbsp white wine vinegar
30 ml / 2 tbsp brandy
15 ml / 1 tbsp plain flour

Set the oven at 190°C / 375°F / gas 5. Weigh the duck and calculate the cooking time at 20 minutes per 450 g / 1 lb. Sprinkle the breast with salt. Put the duck on a wire rack in a roasting tin and prick the skin all over with a fork or skewer to release the fat. Roast for the required time, basting the duck occasionally with the pan juices and pouring away the excess fat as necessary.

Meanwhile, thinly peel the rind from one of the oranges, taking care not to include any of the bitter pith. Cut the rind into strips, then cook these in boiling water for 1 minute. Drain and set aside on absorbent kitchen paper. Slice one of the remaining oranges and set the slices aside for the garnish. Squeeze the rest of the oranges, including the one with the rind removed, and set the juice aside.

Put the sugar in a saucepan with the vinegar. Heat gently, stirring until the sugar has dissolved, then bring to the boil and boil rapidly without stirring until the syrup turns a golden caramel colour. Remove from the heat and carefully add the orange juice and brandy. Return to the heat and stir until just blended, then add the blanched orange rind strips.

When the duck is cooked, transfer it to a platter, remove the trussing string and cut it into serving portions. Transfer to a heated serving dish and keep hot. Pour off the fat from the roasting tin, sprinkle in the flour and cook, stirring, for 2 minutes. Blend in the orange mixture. Bring to the boil, then lower the heat and simmer, stirring, for 3–4 minutes. Add the salt and pepper to taste. Spoon the sauce over the duck, garnish with the reserved orange slices and serve.

SERVES FOUR

FILLETS OF DUCK WITH RICH CHERRY DRESSING

Creamy mashed potatoes or plain cooked noodles and crisp, lightly cooked green beans are suitable accompaniments for this simple, yet rich dish.

4 boneless duck breasts
salt and pepper
2.5 ml / ½ tsp ground mace
4 bay leaves
4 fresh thyme sprigs
125 ml / 4 fl oz red wine
60 ml / 4 tbsp port
25 g / 1 oz butter
15 ml / 1 tbsp finely chopped onion
225 g / 8 oz cherries, stoned
5 ml / 1 tsp grated lemon rind
10 ml / 2 tsp arrowroot

Prick the skin on the duck breasts all over, or remove it, if preferred. Rub plenty of salt, pepper and mace into the breasts, then place them in a shallow dish, skin uppermost, with a bay leaf and thyme sprig under each. Pour the wine and port over the duck, cover and allow to marinate for at least 2 hours; it may be chilled overnight.

Melt the butter in a frying pan and add the onion with the herbs from the duck. Cook over low heat for 5 minutes. Meanwhile, drain the duck breasts, reserving the marinade. Place them skin down in the pan and increase the heat to moderate. Cook until the skin is well browned, then turn the breasts and cook the second side. Allow about 15 minutes on each side to cook the duck breasts.

Using a slotted spoon, transfer the cooked duck to a heated serving dish or individual plates. Keep hot. Leaving the herbs in the pan, add the cherries and lemon rind. Toss the cherries in the cooking juices for about a minute, until the heat causes them to begin to change colour.

Pour in the reserved marinade and heat gently until just boiling. While the sauce is heating, put the arrowroot in a cup and blend to a paste with 15–30 ml / 1–2 tbsp cold water. Add it to the pan, stirring. Bring to the boil and remove the pan from the heat.

Discard the thyme sprigs but arrange the bay leaves on the duck. Use a slotted spoon to divide the cherries between the duck breasts, then pour the sauce over and serve at once.

SERVES FOUR

VARIATION

- **Fillets of Duck Bigarade** Cut the pared rind from 1 Seville orange into fine strips and simmer these in water until tender; drain and set aside. Marinate the duck as above, adding the juice of the orange but omitting the port. Continue as above, stirring 30 ml / 2 tbsp plain flour into the cooking juices from the duck, then add 250 ml / 8 fl oz duck stock or Chicken Stock (page 187) and 5 ml / 1 tsp tomato purée. Bring to the boil, stirring, then add the reserved marinade. Lower the heat and simmer rapidly for 10 minutes. Stir in the juice of ½ lemon and 5 ml / 1 tsp redcurrant jelly. Taste for seasoning and pour over the duck.

MRS BEETON'S TIP

For presentation purposes, cut each cooked duck fillet across into thick slices. Separate the slices slightly on individual plates before finishing with bay leaves, cherries and sauce.

ROAST GOOSE WITH APPLES AND ONIONS

1 goose with giblets
salt and pepper
1 orange
1 lemon
13 small onions
7 bay leaves
1 large fresh thyme sprig
30 ml / 2 tbsp dried sage
1 cinnamon stick
4 cloves
50 g / 2 oz butter
12 Cox's Orange Pippin apples
5 ml / 1 tsp lemon juice
45 ml / 3 tbsp port
45 ml / 3 tbsp crab apple or redcurrant jelly
25 g / 1 oz plain flour

Remove the giblets from the goose and put them in a saucepan. Add 1.5 litres / 2¾ pints water and bring to the boil. Lower the heat and simmer until the liquid is reduced by half. Strain and set aside.

Set the oven at 230°C / 450°F / gas 8. Weigh the goose and calculate the cooking time at 20 minutes per 450 g / 1 lb. Trim away excess fat and rinse the bird, then rub it all over with plenty of salt and pepper. Pare the rind from the fruit and place it in the body cavity with 1 onion, 2 bay leaves and the thyme sprig. Rub the sage over the outside of the bird and tuck a bay leaf behind each of the wing and leg joints.

Place the goose on a rack in a roasting tin. Place it in the oven and immediately reduce the heat to180°C / 350°F / gas 4. Cook for the calculated time, draining away fat from the roasting tin occasionally.

Peel the remaining onions but leave them whole. Place them in a saucepan and pour in boiling water to cover. Add a little salt. Simmer for 15 minutes, then drain well. Squeeze the juice from the orange and lemon, and mix together in a small saucepan. Add the cinnamon, cloves and remaining bay leaf, then heat gently until simmering. Cover and cook for 15 minutes. Remove from the heat and stir in the butter.

Peel and core the apples. As each apple is prepared, place it in a bowl of iced water to which the lemon juice has been added. This will prevent discoloration. Drain the apples, put them in an ovenproof dish and spoon the fruit juice and spice mixture over them to coat them completely. Add the onions, then toss them with the apples so all are coated in juices.

Place the dish of apples and onions in the oven 1 hour before the goose is cooked. Turn them occasionally during cooking so that they are evenly browned and tender. About 10 minutes before the goose is cooked, heat the port and jelly gently in a saucepan or in a bowl in the microwave until the jelly has melted. Spoon this over the apple and onion mixture for the final 5 minutes.

When the goose is cooked, transfer it to a heated serving platter and keep hot. Drain off the fat from the tin. Stir the flour into the cooking juices and cook over low heat for 5 minutes, scraping in all the sediment from the base of the pan. Pour in the reserved giblet stock and bring to the boil, stirring all the time. Taste for seasoning and pour or strain into a sauceboat.

Serve the goose surrounded by the glazed apples and onions, with their juices

SERVES SIX
(WITH MEAT TO SPARE, DEPENDING ON THE SIZE OF THE GOOSE)

ROAST RIBS OF BEEF WITH YORKSHIRE PUDDING

This impressive joint is also known as a standing rib roast. Ask the butcher to trim the thin ends of the bones so that the joint will stand upright. The recipe below, as in Mrs Beeton's day, uses clarified dripping for cooking, but the roast may be cooked without any additional fat, if preferred. There will be sufficient fat from the meat for basting.

2.5 kg / 5½ lb forerib of beef
50–75 g / 2–3 oz beef dripping
salt and pepper
Vegetable Stock (page 188) or water (see method)

YORKSHIRE PUDDING
100 g / 4 oz plain flour
1 egg, beaten
150 ml / ¼ pint milk

Set the oven at 230°C / 450°F / gas 8. Wipe the meat but do not salt it. Melt 50 g / 2 oz of the dripping in a roasting tin, add the meat and quickly spoon some of the hot fat over it. Roast for 10 minutes.

Lower the oven temperature to 180°C / 350°F / gas 4. Baste the meat thoroughly, then continue to roast for a further 1¾ hours for rare meat; 2¼ hours for well-done meat. Baste frequently during cooking.

Meanwhile make the Yorkshire pudding batter. Sift the flour into a bowl and add a pinch of salt. Make a well in the centre of the flour and add the beaten egg. Stir in the milk, gradually working in the flour. Beat vigorously until the mixture is smooth and bubbly, then stir in 150 ml / ¼ pint water.

About 30 minutes before the end of the cooking time, spoon off 30 ml / 2 tbsp of the dripping and divide it between six 7.5-cm / 3-inch Yorkshire pudding tins. Place the tins in the oven for 5 minutes or until the fat is very hot, then carefully divide the batter between them. Bake above the meat for 15–20 minutes.

When the beef is cooked, salt it lightly, transfer it to a warmed serving platter and keep hot. Pour off almost all the water in the roasting tin, leaving the sediment. Pour in enough vegetable stock or water to make a thin gravy, then heat to boiling point, stirring all the time. Season with salt and pepper and serve in a heated gravyboat with the roast beef and Yorkshire puddings.

SERVES SIX TO EIGHT

MRS BEETON'S TIP

Yorkshire pudding is traditionally cooked in a large tin below the joint, so that some of the cooking juices from the meat fall into the pudding to give it an excellent flavour. In a modern oven, this means using a rotisserie or resting the meat directly on the oven shelf. The pudding should be cooked in a large roasting tin, then cut into portions and served as a course on its own before the meat course. Gravy should be poured over the portions of pudding.

CHÂTEAUBRIAND STEAK

Châteaubriand is a luxury cut, from the thickest part of the beef fillet.

1 double fillet steak, not less than
4 cm / 1½ inches thick, trimmed
melted butter
freshly ground black pepper
maîtré d'hôtel butter (see Mrs Beeton's Tip)
or Béarnaise Sauce (page 191) to serve

Brush the steak generously all over with melted butter, season with pepper and place on a rack in a grill pan. Cook under a very hot grill for 2–3 minutes until browned and sealed. Turn the steak over, using a palette knife or spoons, and grill until browned. Lower the heat slightly and continue grilling, turning the steak once or twice, until cooked to taste. Rare meat will require a total cooking time of about 20 minutes; for medium-rare add an extra 5 minutes.

Cut the meat downwards at a slight angle into four even slices. Put two slices on each of two heated plates, top with maître d'hôtel butter or Béarnaise Sauce and serve at once.

SERVES TWO

MRS BEETON'S TIP

To make maître d'hôtel butter, beat 100 g / 4 oz butter until creamy in a small bowl. Finely chop 4–5 large sprigs of parsley and add them to the butter a little at a time, beating until well combined. Add salt to taste and a small pinch of pepper, then add a few drops of lemon juice to intensify the flavour. Use at once or press into small pots, tapping the pots while filling to knock out all the air. Cover with foil and refrigerate until required. Use within 2 days.

TOURNEDOS ROSSINI

Tournedos is a slice from the fillet, usually about 2 cm / ¾ inch thick and a neat round shape. In the classic version of this recipe, foie gras and truffles are used instead of liver pâté and mushrooms, and the dish is served with a brown sauce enriched with Madeira.

4 x 175 g / 6 oz tournedos steaks, trimmed
4 slices of white bread
100 g / 4 oz butter
15 ml / 1 tbsp cooking oil
salt and pepper

GARNISH
4 rounds of good quality liver pâté, 5 mm / ¼ inch thick
4 small flat mushrooms
20 ml / 4 tsp chilled butter
watercress sprigs

Tie the tournedos to a neat shape. Cut the bread slices into 4 rounds, each large enough to accommodate one of the steaks. Melt half the butter in the oil in a large, deep frying pan and fry the bread rounds over moderate heat until pale gold and crisp on both sides. Transfer to a warmed serving dish, cover with buttered greaseproof paper and keep warm.

Add half the remaining butter to the pan. When hot, add the steaks to the pan and fry quickly for 2–3 minutes on each side, or until well seared and browned all over, but rare inside. Remove them from the pan, using a palette knife or two spoons, and place one on each fried bread round. Keep hot.

Heat the remaining butter in a small frying pan, add the pâté slices and mushrooms and turn over high heat until the mushrooms are soft and the pâté is lightly browned but still holds its shape.

Place a slice of pâté on each tournedos and cap it with a mushroom, gill side down. Top each mushroom with 5 ml / 1 tsp chilled butter. Garnish with watercress and serve at once, with freshly ground black pepper.

SERVES FOUR

SCOTCH COLLOPS

Collop is said to be derived from escalope, meaning slice. It was also used as an everyday term for veal, so sliced veal could equally well have been used in this old-fashioned dish. Minced collops, a less extravagant variation on this recipe, uses hand-minced, or diced steak in place of sliced meat.

50 g / 2 oz dripping, lard or butter
675 g / 1½ lb rump steak, beaten and cut into thin slices, about 7.5 cm / 3 inches long
25 g / 1 oz plain flour
salt and pepper
½ small onion or 1 shallot, finely chopped
250 ml / 8 fl oz good beef stock
5 ml / 1 tsp chopped capers
1 pickled walnut, chopped

Heat the fat in a deep frying pan. In a bowl or stout polythene bag, toss the meat with the flour, salt and pepper, then add the slices to the hot fat and fry until browned on all sides. With a slotted spoon, remove the meat from the pan.

Add the onion or shallot to the fat remaining in the pan and fry gently until softened but not browned. Stir in any flour left from dusting the meat and cook for about 5 minutes, stirring all the time, until the flour begins to brown.

Gradually add the stock, stirring constantly, then add the capers, pickled walnut and salt and pepper to taste. Bring to the boil, stirring constantly, then lower the heat and replace the meat. Simmer very gently for 10 minutes and serve hot.

SERVES FOUR TO SIX

VARIATION

- **Minced Collops** Braising steak may be used instead of rump. Trim and chop the meat by hand (minced beef is too fine) – it should be finely chopped. Use 1 chopped onion and fry it in the fat, then add the beef tossed in flour, and cook until browned. Add the stock and seasoning, as above, without removing the meat from the pan. Omit the capers and walnut but add a bouquet garni and a dash of Worcestershire sauce or mushroom ketchup instead. Bring just to the boil, then cover and simmer gently for 1–1½ hours, until tender. Garnish with sippets (see page 59).

STEAK AU POIVRE

20 ml / 4 tsp whole black and white peppercorns, mixed
4 x 150–200 g / 5–7 oz steaks (fillet, sirloin or entrecôte), wiped and trimmed
1 garlic clove, cut in half
60 ml / 4 tbsp olive oil
50 g / 2 oz butter

PARSLEY BUTTER

50 g / 2 oz butter, softened
30 ml / 2 tbsp chopped parsley
salt and pepper

Make the parsley butter. Beat the butter until creamy in a small bowl. Add the parsley, beating until well combined, then season the mixture with salt and a small pinch of pepper. Form into a roll, wrap in greaseproof paper, and refrigerate until required.

Crush the peppercorns in a mortar with a pestle. Set aside. Rub the steaks on both sides with the cut clove of garlic, then brush both sides generously with olive oil. With the heel of your hand, press the crushed peppercorns into the surface of the meat on each side.

Melt the butter with any remaining olive oil in a heavy-bottomed frying pan. When hot, add the steaks to the pan and fry quickly on both sides, allowing 2–3 minutes a side for rare steak; 3½–4 minutes for medium-rare and 5–6 minutes a side for well done. Using a palette knife or two spoons, transfer the steaks to a warmed serving dish. Slice the parsley butter into rounds and place one on top of each steak. Serve at once.

SERVES FOUR

BEEF OLIVES

This makes an excellent main course for a casual dinner party and has the advantage that the meat is prepared in individual portions and needs very little last-minute attention.

450 g / 1 lb rump or chuck steak, trimmed
45 ml / 3 tbsp dripping or oil
1 large onion, sliced
45 ml / 3 tbsp plain flour
600 ml / 1 pint beef stock
1 tomato, peeled and sliced
1 carrot, sliced
15 ml / 1 tbsp Worcestershire sauce
salt and pepper
30 ml / 2 tbsp chopped parsley
fresh herb sprigs to garnish

STUFFING
50 g / 2 oz margarine
100 g / 4 oz fresh white breadcrumbs
pinch of grated nutmeg
15 ml / 1 tbsp chopped parsley
5 ml / 1 tsp chopped fresh mixed herbs
grated rind of ½ lemon
1 egg, beaten

Make the stuffing. Melt the margarine in a small saucepan. Add the breadcrumbs, nutmeg, herbs and lemon rind, with salt and pepper to taste. Add enough beaten egg to bind the mixture.

Cut the meat into four slices and flatten each with a cutlet bat or rolling pin. Divide the stuffing between the meat slices, spreading it out evenly. Roll each piece of meat up tightly and tie securely with fine string or cotton.

Heat the dripping or oil in a large saucepan and fry the beef olives, turning them frequently until browned. Using a slotted spoon, transfer them to a plate.

Add the onion slices to the fat remaining in the pan and fry until golden brown. Using a slotted spoon, transfer to the plate with the beef olives. Add the flour to the pan and cook until golden brown, stirring constantly. Gradually add the stock, stirring until the mixture boils, then lower the heat and simmer for 5 minutes.

Return the beef olives and onion slices to the pan. Add the tomato, carrot and Worcestershire sauce, with salt and pepper to taste. Cover the pan with a tight-fitting lid and simmer for 1–2 hours.

Having removed the strings from the beef olives, serve them on a bed of mashed potato or rice. Strain the sauce and pour it over the beef olives. Sprinkle with chopped parsley and garnish with fresh herbs (the same types as used in the stuffing). Serve at once.

SERVES FOUR

VARIATIONS

- **Hanover Rouladen** Omit the stuffing. Instead lay a strip of gherkin on each portion of beef, with 15 ml / 1 tbsp finely chopped onion, 15 ml / 1 tbsp chopped ham and 5 ml / 1 tsp capers. Proceed as in the recipe above but cook for 1½ hours only.
- **Mushroom Paupiettes** Use a mushroom stuffing instead of herb. Chop 1 rindless bacon rasher and fry without additional fat for 2 minutes. Add 100 g / 4 oz finely chopped mushrooms and fry over gentle heat for 5 minutes, stirring. Stir in 100 g / 4 oz fresh white breadcrumbs, a knob of butter and pinch of grated nutmeg. Add salt and pepper to taste. Bind with beaten egg. Prepare and cook the paupiettes as for the beef olives in the recipe above, but stir 250 ml / 8 fl oz soured cream into the sauce just before serving.

BEEF STROGANOFF

675 g / 1½ lb thinly sliced rump steak, trimmed
45 ml / 3 tbsp plain flour
salt and pepper
50 g / 2 oz butter
225 g / 8 oz onions, thinly sliced
225 g / 8 oz mushrooms, thinly sliced
250 ml / 8 fl oz soured cream

Beat the steak slices with a cutlet bat or rolling pin, then cut them into thin strips. Put the flour in a shallow bowl, season with plenty of salt and pepper and coat the beef strips.

Melt half the butter in a large heavy-bottomed saucepan, add the onion slices and fry for about 10 minutes until golden. Stir in the mushrooms and continue cooking for a further 2–3 minutes. Using a slotted spoon, transfer the vegetables to a dish. Set aside.

Melt the remaining butter in the pan, add the meat and fry rapidly for 2–3 minutes, turning frequently. Return the vegetables to the pan and heat through for 1 minute. Pour in the soured cream, stir once or twice, and heat for 1–2 minutes until all the ingredients are heated through (see Mrs Beeton's Tip). Serve at once, with noodles, boiled new potatoes or rice.

SERVES FOUR

MRS BEETON'S TIP

Do not allow the sauce to approach boiling point after the soured cream has been added, or it will curdle.

GOULASH

It is the paprika that gives this hearty Hungarian stew its delicious flavour. Serve simply, with crusty bread.

50 g / 2 oz dripping or lard
675 g / 1½ lb chuck or blade steak, trimmed and cut into 2-cm / ¾-inch cubes
2 onions, sliced
30 ml / 2 tbsp plain flour
125 ml / 4 fl oz beef stock
125 ml / 4 fl oz red wine
450 g / 1 lb tomatoes, peeled and diced or 1 x 397 g / 14 oz can chopped tomatoes
2.5 ml / ½ tsp salt
15 ml / 1 tbsp paprika
1 bouquet garni
450 g / 1 lb potatoes
150 ml / ¼ pint soured cream

Heat the dripping in a flameproof casserole and fry the meat until browned on all sides. Using a slotted spoon, remove the meat and set aside. Add the onions to the fat remaining in the casserole and fry gently until just beginning to brown. Add the flour and cook, stirring until browned. Gradually add the stock and wine, with the tomatoes, salt, paprika and bouquet garni. Bring to the boil, stirring, then lower the heat and simmer for 1½–2 hours or until the meat is tender. Alternatively, transfer the goulash to a casserole and bake at 160°C / 325°F / gas 3 for 1½–2 hours.

Thirty minutes before the end of the cooking time, peel the potatoes, cut them into cubes and add them to the goulash. When cooked they should be tender but not broken. Just before serving, remove the bouquet garni and stir in the soured cream.

SERVES SIX

CARBONNADE OF BEEF

Brown ale and long, slow cooking combine to make this classic, full-flavoured stew with its crunchy topping of mustard-seasoned French bread.

50 g / 2 oz butter or margarine
675 g / 1½ lb stewing steak, trimmed and cut into 4 cm / 1½ inch cubes
2 large onions, sliced
1 garlic clove, crushed
15 ml / 1 tbsp plain flour
250 ml / 8 fl oz beef stock
375 ml / 13 fl oz brown ale
salt and pepper
1 bouquet garni
pinch of grated nutmeg
pinch of soft light brown sugar
5 ml / 1 tsp red wine vinegar
6 thin slices of French bread
15 ml / 1 tbsp French mustard

Set the oven at 160°C / 325°F / gas 3. Melt the butter or margarine in a heavy-bottomed frying pan, add the beef and fry quickly until browned on all sides. Using a slotted spoon, transfer the beef to a casserole and keep hot. Add the onions to the fat remaining in the pan and fry until lightly browned, then stir in the garlic and fry over gentle heat for 1 minute.

Pour off any excess fat from the pan, leaving about 15 ml / 1 tbsp. Add the flour to the onions and garlic and cook, stirring constantly, until lightly browned.

PRESSURE COOKER TIP

Follow the recipe above, removing the open pressure cooker from the heat before adding the stock and ale. The cooker should not be more than half full. Close the cooker, bring to 15 lb pressure and cook for 20 minutes. Reduce the pressure quickly. Transfer the stew to a casserole, top with the bread slices as left, and grill until golden.

Gradually stir in the stock and ale, with salt and pepper to taste. Add the bouquet garni, nutmeg, brown sugar and vinegar. Bring to the boil, then pour the liquid over the beef in the casserole. Cover and bake for 1½–2 hours or until the beef is tender. Remove the bouquet garni.

Spread the French bread slices with mustard. Arrange them, mustard side up, on top of the carbonnade, pressing them down so that they absorb the gravy. Return the casserole to the oven, uncovered, for about 15 minutes or until the bread browns slightly. Alternatively, place under a hot grill for a few minutes. Serve immediately, straight from the casserole.

SERVES SIX

BAKED STUFFED PEPPERS

oil for greasing
4 green peppers
1 small onion, finely chopped
400 g / 14 oz lean minced beef
100 g / 4 oz cooked rice
salt and pepper
good pinch of dried marjoram
250 ml / 8 fl oz tomato juice
strips of green pepper to garnish

Grease an ovenproof dish. Set the oven at 180°C / 350°F / gas 4. Cut a slice off the top of each pepper, then remove the membranes and seeds. Blanch in a saucepan of boiling water for 2 minutes.

Mix the onion, beef, rice, salt, pepper and marjoram together in a bowl. Stand the peppers upright in the prepared dish; if they do not stand upright easily, cut a thin slice off the base. Divide the stuffing mixture between the peppers. Pour the tomato juice around the base of the peppers. Cover and bake for 1 hour. Garnish with strips of pepper.

SERVES FOUR

BEEF AND POTATO PIE

This is simple country cooking with no frills. Salt and pepper are the only condiments used; the pie deriving its flavour from long slow cooking of meat and vegetables. It is therefore important that the stewing steak is of good quality. Remember that stewing steak gives a better flavour than braising steak in a recipe of this type.

675 g / 1½ lb stewing steak trimmed and cut into 2-cm / ¾-inch cubes
3 onions, sliced
3 large carrots, sliced
1 kg / 2¼ lb potatoes, sliced
salt and pepper
hot beef stock (see method)

Set the oven at 160°C / 325°F / gas 3. Layer the meat with the onion, carrot and potato slices in an ovenproof casserole, finishing with a neat layer of potatoes. Add salt and pepper.

Pour in enough hot stock to three-quarters cover the contents of the casserole, reserving some stock for adding if the dish begins to dry out during cooking. Cover with a tight-fitting lid or foil and bake for 3–3½ hours, or until the beef is very tender. About 30–40 minutes before the end of the cooking time, remove the casserole lid to allow the top layer of potato to brown. Serve straight from the casserole.

SERVES SIX

MRS BEETON'S TIP

If liked, the top layer of potato may be sprinked with paprika before browning. Use a sweet Hungarian rose paprika if possible.

ROAST RACK OF LAMB

1 rack of lamb
45 ml / 3 tbsp plain flour
salt and pepper
30 ml / 2 tbsp redcurrant jelly

Set the oven at 180°C / 350°F / gas 4. Weigh the joint of lamb and calculate the cooking time at 25 minutes per 450 g / 1 lb, plus 25 minutes. This gives a medium result; for a well-done joint allow 30 minutes per 450 g / 1 lb plus 30 minutes.

Dust the joint with flour and plenty of seasoning. Place it in a roasting tin and cook for three-quarters of the time, basting occasionally. Pour off excess fat and pour in 600 ml / 1 pint boiling water. Finish roasting the meat.

Meanwhile, melt the jelly in a small saucepan. Transfer the meat to a serving plate and glaze it with the jelly. Tent with foil to keep hot. Boil the cooking liquor until reduced by about a third, taste for seasoning, pour into a gravyboat and serve with the lamb.

SERVES FOUR TO SIX

VARIATIONS

- **Crown Roast or Guard of Honour** A pair of racks of lamb may be trussed into a crown roast or a guard of honour. For a crown, the racks are sewn end to end, then trussed (sewn) into a ring with the fat side inwards and trimmed bones forming the top of the crown. For a guard of honour, the racks are arranged opposite each other with bone ends interlocked. Both joints are sold ready prepared; both may be stuffed. Stuffing is spooned into the middle of the crown roast or packed between the racks for a guard of honour.

HERBED SHOULDER OF LAMB

This recipe maybe used for leg as well as for shoulder of lamb.

1 shoulder of lamb, boned
4 garlic cloves, peeled and quartered lengthways
about 6 small sprigs each fresh rosemary and thyme
4 bay leaves
2 oranges
60 ml / 4 tbsp olive oil
salt and pepper
300 ml / ½ pint red wine

GARNISH
orange slices
fresh herbs

Trim any lumps of fat from the lamb, then tie it in a neat shape if the butcher has not already done this. Weigh the joint and calculate the cooking time at 30 minutes per 450 g / 1 lb plus 30 minutes. Use a small pointed knife to make short cuts into the lamb, at an angle running under the skin, all over the joint. Insert pieces of garlic and the rosemary and thyme sprigs into the cuts. Place the joint in a deep dish, with two bay leaves underneath and two on top.

Pare two long strips of rind off one orange and add them to the dish, placing them next to or on top of the lamb. Squeeze the juice from the oranges, then mix it with the olive oil, salt and pepper. Pour this mixture over the lamb, cover and marinate for several hours or overnight. Turn the joint at least once during the marinating time.

Set the oven at 180°C / 350°F / gas 4. Transfer the joint to a roasting tin, adding the bay leaves and orange rind but reserving the marinade. Cook for half the calculated time, brushing occasionally with the reserved marinade and basting with cooking juices from the tin. Pour the remaining marinade and the wine over the joint and continue roasting. Baste the lamb occasionally and add a little water to the juices in the tin if they begin to dry up – if the roasting tin is large they will evaporate more speedily.

Transfer the cooked joint to a serving dish, cover with foil and set aside. Pour 300 ml / ½ pint boiling water or vegetable cooking water into the roasting tin. Boil the cooking juices rapidly, stirring and scraping the sediment off the base and sides of the pan, until they are reduced by half. Taste for seasoning, then strain the sauce into a heated sauceboat.

Garnish the lamb with orange slices and fresh herbs and serve at once, carving it into thick slices. Offer the sauce separately.

SERVES SIX

MRS BEETON'S TIP

Once it has been reduced, the sauce may be thickened by whisking in small knobs of beurre manié, then boiling for 2 minutes, whisking all the time. To make beurre manié cream 25 g / 1 oz butter with 30–45 ml / 2–3 tbsp plain flour.

LOIN OF LAMB WITH LEMON AND PARSLEY STUFFING

Adapted from one of Mrs Beeton's first edition recipes for a loin of mutton, this lightly spiced roast joint was originally part baked and part stewed. It was justifiably described as 'very excellent'. The same combination of ingredients and stuffing will complement a leg or shoulder joint.

1 x 1.4–1.6 kg / 3–3½ lb boned and rolled double loin of lamb, bones reserved, trimmed
salt and pepper
1.25 ml / ¼ tsp each ground allspice and mace, and grated nutmeg
6 cloves
600 ml / 1 pint lamb, Chicken (page 187) or Vegetable Stock (page 188)
30 ml / 2 tbsp plain flour
25 g / 1 oz butter
125 ml / 4 fl oz port
30 ml / 2 tbsp mushroom ketchup
100 g / 4 oz button mushrooms, sliced

STUFFING

50 g / 2 oz shredded beef suet
50 g / 2 oz cooked ham, chopped
15 ml / 1 tbsp finely chopped parsley
5 ml / 1 tsp chopped fresh thyme
grated rind of ½ lemon
175 g / 6 oz fresh white breadcrumbs
2.5 ml / ½ tsp grated nutmeg or ground mace
pinch of cayenne pepper
1 egg, beaten
a little milk

Open out the lamb and sprinkle the inside lightly with salt and pepper. Mix the allspice, mace and nutmeg, then rub the spices all over the meat, both outside and on the cut surface. Cover and allow to marinate for at least 1 hour, or up to 24 hours.

Make the stuffing. Combine the suet, ham, parsley, thyme, lemon rind, breadcrumbs and nutmeg or mace in a bowl. Add salt and pepper to taste, and the cayenne. Stir in the egg and add enough milk to bind the mixture lightly together. Spread the stuffing evenly over the inside of the lamb, carefully roll it up again and tie it neatly. Stick the cloves into the joint, piercing it first with the point of a knife.

Set the oven at 180°C / 350°F / gas 4. Put the lamb bones in the bottom of a roasting tin and pour over just enough stock to cover them. Weigh the meat and calculate the cooking time. Allow 30 minutes per 450 g / 1 lb plus 30 minutes over. Place the stuffed lamb on top of the bones in the tin. Cook for the calculated time, adding extra stock or water during cooking to maintain the level of liquid just below the top of the bones and. joint. Baste the joint occasionally with the cooking juices.

When the lamb is cooked, transfer it to a heated serving platter and allow to rest under tented foil. Remove the bones and skim off most of the fat from the liquid in the roasting tin. Beat the flour and butter to a smooth paste. Place the roasting liquid over medium heat, stir in the port and mushroom ketchup, then bring the mixture to simmering point. Whisking all the time, gradually add small lumps of the butter and flour mixture. Continue whisking well after each addition, until the sauce boils and thickens. Stir in the mushrooms and simmer for 3 minutes.

Taste the sauce for seasoning before serving it with the lamb, which should be carved into thick slices. Redcurrant jelly, new potatoes and fresh peas are excellent accompaniments.

SERVES SIX

LAMB CUTLETS EN PAPILLOTE

oil for greasing
4–6 slices of cooked ham
6 lamb cutlets, trimmed
15 ml / 1 tbsp oil
1 onion, finely chopped
25 g / 1 oz button mushrooms, finely chopped
10 ml / 2 tsp finely chopped parsley
grated rind of ½ lemon
salt and pepper

Set the oven at 190°C / 375°F / gas 5. Cut out 12 small rounds of ham, each large enough to cover the round part of a cutlet. Heat the oil in a small saucepan and fry the onion for 4–6 minutes until slightly softened. Remove from the heat and stir in the mushrooms, parsley and lemon rind, with salt and pepper to taste. Leave to cool.

Cut out six heart-shaped pieces of double thickness greaseproof paper or foil large enough to hold the cutlets. Grease the paper generously with oil. Centre one of the ham rounds on the right half of one of the prepared paper hearts, spread with a little of the mushroom mixture and lay a cutlet on top. Spread the cutlet with a little more of the mushroom mixture and add another round of ham so that the round part of the cutlet is neatly sandwiched. Fold over the paper and twist the edges well together.

Lay the wrapped cutlets on a greased baking sheet and bake for 30 minutes. Transfer, still in their wrappings, to heated individual plates and serve at once.

SERVES SIX

NOISETTES JARDINIÈRE

1 kg / 2¼ lb boned best end of neck of lamb
30 ml / 2 tbsp oil
salt and pepper
50 g / 2 oz green beans, diced
1 carrot, diced
1 small turnip, diced
2 celery sticks, diced
450 g / 1 lb potatoes, halved and cooked
25 g / 1 oz butter
15–30 ml / 2–3 tbsp single cream
gravy to serve

Wipe the meat. Roll it up and tie with fine string at 2.5-cm / 1-inch intervals. Cut through the roll between the string.

Brush the noisettes with oil, season generously with salt and pepper and cook for 6–7 minutes under a moderate grill until cooked through and browned on both sides. Meanwhile, cook each vegetable except the potatoes separately in boiling salted water until just tender. Drain and mix.

Mash the potatoes until smooth. Beat in the butter and single cream. Spoon the creamed potato into a piping bag fitted with a large star nozzle and pipe a border of mashed potato around the edge of a heated serving dish. Arrange the noisettes and vegetables on the dish. Serve at once with hot gravy made using the cooking juices.

SERVES SIX

MRS BEETON'S TIP

If preferred, the noisettes may be cooked in a frying pan. Heat the oil, add the noisettes and fry for about 3 minutes on each side.

SHEPHERD'S PIE

butter for greasing
50 g / 2 oz butter
2 onions, roughly chopped
15 ml / 1 tbsp plain flour
250 ml / 8 fl oz well-flavoured lamb stock
575 g / 1¼ lb lean cooked lamb, minced
salt and pepper
5 ml / 1 tsp Worcestershire sauce
675 g / 1½ 1b potatoes, halved
15–30 ml / 1–2 tbsp milk
pinch of grated nutmeg

Melt half the butter in a saucepan and fry the onions until softened but not coloured. Stir in the flour and cook gently for 1–2 minutes, stirring all the time. Gradually add the stock. Bring to the boil, stirring until the sauce thickens.

Stir in the lamb, with salt and pepper and Worcestershire sauce to taste. Cover the pan and simmer for 30 minutes.

Meanwhile cook the potatoes in a saucepan of salted boiling water for about 30 minutes or until tender. Drain thoroughly and mash with a potato masher, or beat them with a hand-held electric whisk until smooth. Beat in the rest of the butter and the milk to make a creamy consistency. Add salt, pepper and nutmeg to taste.

Set the oven at 220°C / 450°F / gas 7. Spoon the meat mixture into a greased pie dish or shallow oven-to-table dish. Cover with the potato, smooth the top, then flick it up into small peaks or score a pattern on the surface with a fork. Bake for 10–15 minutes until browned on top. Serve at once.

SERVES FOUR TO SIX

LAMB SHASHLIK

50 g / 2 oz butter
450 g / 1 lb boned leg of lamb, cut into 2-cm / 1-inch cubes
200 g / 7 oz lean bacon, cut into 1-cm / ½-inch cubes
8 button onions
8 bay leaves
salt and pepper

Heat 25 g / 1 oz of the butter in a large frying pan, add the lamb cubes and brown on all sides. Bring a small saucepan of water to the boil, add the onions and cook for 3 minutes; drain thoroughly.

Divide the meat, bacon, onions and bay leaves into 4 portions. Thread each portion on to a long skewer. Season with salt and pepper. Melt the remaining butter in a small pan and brush the meat and vegetables generously all over.

Cook the shashlik under a hot grill or over medium coals for 8–10 minutes, turning the skewers occasionally, until the meat is well browned. Serve with rice and Cucumber in Yogurt (page 39).

SERVES FOUR

LAMB CURRY

1 kg / 2¼ lb boneless leg or shoulder lamb, cut into 2.5-cm / 1-inch cubes
60 ml / 4 tbsp lemon juice
450 ml / ¾ pint plain yogurt
salt and freshly ground black pepper
75 g / 3 oz clarified butter (see Mrs Beeton's Tip page 165)
2 onions, finely chopped
3 garlic cloves, crushed
5 cm / 2 inch fresh root ginger, grated
5 ml / 1 tsp chilli powder
10 ml / 2 tsp each ground coriander and cumin
8 green cardamom pods
150 g / 5 oz tomato purée

Put the lamb cubes into a large non-metallic bowl and sprinkle with the lemon juice. Stir in the yogurt and salt. Cover and marinate for 24 hours or for up to 3 days. Stir the mixture occasionally.

Heat the ghee in a large saucepan, add the onions, garlic and ginger and fry for 4–6 minutes until the onion is soft but not coloured. Add the chilli powder, coriander, cumin and black pepper and fry for 2 minutes, then stir in the lamb, with its marinade. Stir in the cardamom pods and tomato purée, with 300 ml / ½ pint water. Bring to the boil, reduce the heat and simmer for about 1 hour or until the meat is tender. Serve with rice, chopped tomato and onion, and Cucumber in Yogurt (page 39).

SERVES FOUR TO SIX

MOUSSAKA

oil for greasing
1 aubergine
salt and pepper
30 ml / 2 tbsp olive oil
1 large onion, chopped
1 garlic clove, crushed
450 g / 1 lb minced lamb or beef
10 ml / 2 tsp chopped parsley
2 tomatoes, peeled, seeded and chopped
150 ml / ¼ pint dry white wine
300 ml / ½ pint milk
1 egg, plus 2 egg yolks
pinch of grated nutmeg
75 g / 3 oz Kefalotiri or Parmesan cheese, grated

Grease a 20 x 10 x 10-cm (8 x 4 x 4-inch) baking dish. Set the oven at 180°C / 350°F / gas 4. Cut the aubergine into 1 cm / ½ inch slices, put them in a colander, and sprinkle generously with salt. Set aside.

Heat the olive oil, and gently fry the onion and garlic for about 10 minutes until the onion is soft. Add the mince and continue cooking, stirring with a fork to break up any lumps in the meat. When the meat is thoroughly browned, add salt, pepper, parsley and tomatoes. Mix well, then add the white wine.

In a bowl, beat together the milk, whole egg, egg yolks, salt and a good pinch of grated nutmeg. Add about half the grated cheese to the egg mixture, then beat again briefly.

Rinse and drain the aubergine slices and pat dry with absorbent kitchen paper. Place half in the bottom of the prepared dish and cover with the meat mixture. Lay the remaining aubergine slices on the meat and pour the milk and egg mixture over them. Sprinkle the remaining cheese on top. Bake for 30–40 minutes, until golden brown.

SERVES FOUR

ROAST PORK WITH MUSHROOM AND CORN STUFFING

If the whole joint is served at the table, you may like to add a garnish of baby sweetcorn cobs (cook them in boiling water for 3–5 minutes) and button mushrooms tossed in hot butter.

1.5 kg / 3 lb boned bladebone of pork, scored (see Mrs Beeton's Tip)
45 ml / 3 tbsp oil
15 ml / 1 tbsp cooking salt

STUFFING
25 g / 1 oz butter or margarine
1 onion, finely chopped
1 celery stick, finely chopped
100 g / 4 oz mushrooms, finely chopped
50 g / 2 oz thawed frozen sweetcorn, drained
50 g / 2 oz fresh white breadcrumbs
15 ml / 1 tbsp chopped parsley
2.5 ml / ½ tsp ground mace
5 ml / 1 tsp lemon juice
salt and pepper

Set the oven at 230°C / 450°F / gas 8. Make the stuffing. Melt the butter or margarine in a small saucepan, then add the onion and celery and fry for 4–6 minutes until soft but not browned. Remove from the heat and add the remaining ingredients.

Spoon the stuffing evenly into the 'pocket' left when the meat was boned. Roll up the joint and tie with thin string at regular intervals. Generously brush 15 ml / 1 tbsp of the oil over the rind. Sprinkle with the salt, rubbing it well in.

Heat the remaining oil in a roasting tin, add the meat, turning it in the hot fat, and roast for 20–30 minutes until the crackling crisps. Do not cover the meat or the crackling will soften again. Lower the heat to 180°C / 350°F / gas 4 and cook for about 1[and one half] hours more or until the pork is cooked.

Transfer the meat to a warmed serving dish, remove the string and keep hot. If liked, pour off the fat from the roasting tin, using the sediment for gravy (see page 184).

SERVES SIX

MRS BEETON'S TIP

If the butcher has not already scored the pork rind, do this yourself, using a very sharp knife and making the cuts about 3 mm / ⅛ inch deep and 1 cm / ½ inch apart.

SAVOURY LOIN OF PORK

1–1.5 kg / 2¼–3¼ lb loin of pork on the bone
15 ml / 1 tbsp finely chopped onion
2.5 ml / ½ tsp dried sage
2.5 ml / ½ tsp salt
1.25 ml / ¼ tsp freshly ground pepper
pinch of dry mustard
30 ml / 2 tbsp sieved apricot jam, melted
125 ml / 4 fl oz Apple Sauce (page 198)

Set the oven at 220°C / 425°F / gas 7. Weigh the meat and calculate the cooking time at 30 minutes per 450 g / 1 lb plus 30 minutes over. Mix the onion, sage, salt, pepper and mustard in a small bowl. Rub the mixture well into the surface of the meat.

Put the meat in a roasting tin and roast for 10 minutes, then lower the oven temperature to 180°C / 350°F / gas 4 and roast for the remainder of the calculated cooking time. About 30 minutes before serving, remove the pork from the oven and brush with melted apricot jam. Continue cooking to crisp the crackling.

Serve the pork on a heated serving dish, offering the Apple Sauce separately.

SERVES SIX

MRS BEETON'S TIP

If a savoury glaze is preferred for the crackling, brush with oil and sprinkle with salt. Raise the oven temperature to 220°C / 425°F / gas 7, return the pork to the oven and continue cooking for 15–20 minutes.

CIDERED PORK CHOPS

4 pork loin chops, trimmed
oil (see method)
60 ml / 4 tbsp dry cider
1 bouquet garni
2 cooking apples
2 onions, chopped
pinch of ground cinnamon
salt and pepper
100 g / 4 oz flat mushrooms, thickly sliced
200 g / 7 oz fresh peas
25 g / 1 oz butter
200 g / 7 oz cooked small whole beetroot
225 g / 8 oz tagliatelle, cooked

Set the oven at 160°C / 325°F / gas 3. Heat a frying pan. Brown the chops on both sides, adding a little oil if the chops are very lean. Remove the chops and place them in a casserole. Pour the cider over the chops and add the bouquet garni. Cover the casserole and start cooking it in the oven.

Peel, core and chop the apples. Add them with the onions to the fat remaining in the frying pan and fry gently for 5 minutes. Stir in the cinnamon, with just enough water to cover the onion mixture. Cover the pan and simmer for about 15 minutes, until the onions and apples are soft. Rub the mixture through a sieve into a bowl, add salt and pepper to taste, then spoon the mixture over the chops in the casserole. Return to the oven for 45 minutes.

Add the mushrooms and peas to the casserole and cook for 30 minutes more. Towards the end of the cooking time, melt the butter in a small saucepan, add the beetroot and heat gently, turning often. Arrange the tagliatelle and chops on a heated serving dish with the chops on top. Arrange the mushrooms, peas and beetroot around them.

SERVES FOUR

BARBECUED SPARE RIBS

2 kg / 4½ lb pork spare ribs
1 lemon, cut in wedges
herb sprigs to garnish (optional)

BARBECUE SPICE MIXTURE
90 ml / 6 tbsp soft light brown sugar
15 ml / 1 tbsp grated lemon rind
15 ml / 1 tbsp paprika
salt and pepper

BASTING SAUCE
200 ml / 7 fl oz tomato juice
45 ml / 3 tbsp tomato ketchup
15–30 ml / 1–2 tbsp Worcestershire sauce
30 ml / 2 tbsp soft light brown sugar
5 ml / 1 tsp mustard powder
1.25 ml / ¼ tsp chilli powder

Cut the ribs into individual portions. Mix all the ingredients for the barbecue spice mixture and rub into the ribs.

Meanwhile make the basting sauce. Combine all the ingredients in a small saucepan. Add 100 ml / 3½ fl oz water, bring to the boil, then lower the heat and simmer for 15 minutes. Spread out the ribs in a large shallow dish or roasting tin and brush generously with the basting sauce. Cover and set aside for 30 minutes at cool room temperature. Brush again and leave for a further 30 minutes.

Cook the ribs on a grid placed high over medium coals for 1–1¼ hours, turning frequently and basting with the sauce. Alternatively, bake in a preheated 150°C / 300°F / gas 2 oven for about 1 hour or until nearly cooked. Baste frequently. Finish by cooking under a hot grill – or over the fire. Serve with lemon wedges, and garnish with fresh herbs.

SERVES SIX TO EIGHT

TOAD-IN-THE-HOLE

450 g / 1 lb pork sausages

BATTER
100 g / 4 oz plain flour
1.25 ml / ¼ tsp salt
1 egg beaten
300 ml / ½ pint milk, or milk and water

Make the batter. Sift the flour and salt into a bowl, make a well in the centre and add the beaten egg. Stir in half the milk (or all the milk, if using a mixture of milk and water), gradually working in the flour.

Beat vigorously until the mixture is smooth and bubbly, then stir in the rest of the milk (or the water). Pour the batter into a jug and set aside.

Set the oven at 220°C / 425°F / gas 7. Arrange the sausages, spoke-fashion, in a shallow 1.1-litre / 2-pint circular dish. Stand the dish on a baking sheet and cook the sausages for 15 minutes.

Pour the batter over the sausages and bake for a further 40–45 minutes until golden brown and well risen. Serve at once with a rich gravy or home-made tomato sauce.

SERVES FOUR

MARINATED VENISON STEAKS

4 slices of venison (from haunch)
salt and pepper
25 g / 1 oz plain flour
butter or dripping
1 small onion, chopped
6–8 juniper berries, crushed
150 ml / ¼ pint Game or Chicken Stock (page 187)
chopped parsley to garnish

MARINADE

about 300 ml / ½ pint red wine
1 bouquet garni
6 peppercorns
4 onion slices
30 ml / 2 tbsp olive oil
10 ml / 2 tsp red wine vinegar

Make the marinade. Mix all the ingredients in a saucepan and boil for 1 minute. Set aside until completely cool. Put the venison in a large dish. Pour the marinade over; leave overnight.

Set the oven at 180°C / 350°F / gas 4. Drain the venison and pat dry. Reserve the marinade. Snip the edges of the venison slices to prevent curling. Season the flour and rub it over the steaks. Heat the fat in a flameproof casserole. Sear the steaks; add the onion when searing the second side.

Pour off all but a film of fat from the pan. Sprinkle the steaks with the crushed juniper. Pour the stock and a little of the marinade round them, to a depth of about 1 cm / ½ inch. Cover the casserole or tin tightly with foil and bake for 30 minutes, or until the steaks are tender. Drain and serve, sprinkled with parsley. Drain off the excess fat from the stock and serve the stock with the steaks.

SERVES SIX TO EIGHT

BOLOGNESE SAUCE

15 g / ½ oz butter
15 ml / 1 tbsp olive oil
75 g / 3 oz unsmoked rindless streaky bacon rashers, diced
1 onion, finely chopped
2 garlic cloves, crushed
1 carrot, finely diced
½ celery stick, thinly sliced
225 g / 8 oz lean minced beef
100 g / 4 oz chicken livers, trimmed and cut into small shreds
1 x 397 g / 14 oz can chopped tomatoes
200 ml / 7 fl oz beef stock
15 ml / 1 tbsp tomato purée
125 ml / 4 fl oz dry white or red wine
5 ml / 1 tsp dried marjoram
salt and pepper
pinch of grated nutmeg

Melt the butter in the oil in a saucepan. Add the bacon and cook it gently until brown. Add the onion, garlic, carrot and celery. Cook over gentle heat for about 10 minutes until the onion is soft and just beginning to brown. Add the beef and cook, stirring, until browned and broken up.

Add the chicken livers to the pan and cook for 3 minutes, turning the livers over gently to brown them on all sides. Stir in the tomatoes, stock, tomato purée, wine and marjoram. Add to taste salt, pepper and nutmeg. Bring to simmering point and cook, covered, for about 1 hour, stirring occasionally.

Remove the lid for the final 20 minutes of the cooking time to allow some of the liquid to evaporate. Taste and add extra salt and pepper if necessary. Serve with pasta, rice or baked potatoes.

SERVES FOUR WITH PASTA OR RICE

LASAGNE AL FORNO

150 g / 5 oz lasagne (7 sheets) or
200 g / 7 oz (12 sheets) no-precook lasagne
30 ml / 2 tbsp oil
2 onions, finely chopped
2 garlic cloves, chopped
225 g / 8 oz minced beef
225 g / 8 oz minced pork
100 g / 4 oz mushrooms, sliced
2 x 397 g / 14 oz cans chopped tomatoes
2.5 ml / ½ tsp dried basil
2.5 ml / ½ tsp dried oregano
150 ml / ¼ pint red wine
salt and pepper
900 ml / 1½ pints cold Béchamel Sauce (page 192) or
White Sauce (page 189)
50 g / 2 oz Parmesan cheese, grated

Cook the lasagne, if necessary, in plenty of boiling salted water. Add the lasagne a sheet at a time, then boil for about 12 minutes until tender but not soft. Drain well, rinse under cold water and then lay out to dry on absorbent kitchen paper.

Heat the oil in a heavy-bottomed saucepan, add the onions and garlic and fry over medium heat for 10 minutes. Stir in the beef and pork. Cook, stirring, for 5–10 minutes.

Stir in the mushrooms, tomatoes, herbs and wine. Add salt and pepper. Bring just to the boil, stirring. Reduce the heat, then simmer the sauce steadily, uncovered, stirring occasionally. Allow 1¼–1½ hours until the meat is tender and the sauce thick when stirred.

Set the oven at 180°C / 350°F / gas 4. Spread a thin layer of the white sauce over the base of a 30- x 20-cm / 12- x 8-inch baking dish. Arrange a layer of lasagne in the dish. Top with a layer of meat sauce. Add a thin layer of white sauce, but do not worry too much about spreading the sauce perfectly; the next layer of lasagne will smooth it out. Repeat the layers, ending with white sauce. Sprinkle the top with Parmesan.

Bake for 40–50 minutes, until golden brown. Allow the lasagne to stand for 10 minutes before serving.

SERVES SIX TO EIGHT

STUFFED BAKED CANNELLONI

butter for greasing
12–16 cannelloni
15 ml / 1 tbsp olive oil
300 g / 11 oz frozen chopped spinach
salt and pepper
1.25 ml / ¼ tsp grated nutmeg
150 g / 5 oz ricotta or cottage cheese
50 g / 2 oz cooked ham, finely chopped
600 ml / 1 pint Cheese Sauce (page 189)
25 g / 1 oz dried white breadcrumbs
25 g / 1 oz Parmesan cheese, grated

Butter an ovenproof dish. Set the oven at 180°C / 350°F / gas 4. Cook the cannelloni in a saucepan of boiling salted water with the oil for 10–15 minutes until tender but still firm to the bite. Drain well.

Place the spinach in a saucepan. Cook over low heat for about 10 minutes or until the spinach has thawed completely. Raise the temperature and heat the spinach thoroughly. Drain. Mix the spinach, salt, pepper, nutmeg, soft cheese and ham in a bowl. Spoon the mixture into the cannelloni. Place in the prepared ovenproof dish. Pour the cheese sauce over the cannelloni.

Bake for 15–20 minutes. Mix together the crumbs and Parmesan, then sprinkle over the dish. Place under a hot grill for 2–3 minutes to brown the top.

SERVES FOUR

SPAGHETTI ALLA CARBONARA

450 g / 1 lb spaghetti salt and pepper
15 ml / 1 tbsp oil
100 g / 4 oz rindless streaky bacon rashers, cut into fine strips
4 eggs
30 ml / 2 tbsp double cream
75 g / 3 oz Pecorino or Parmesan cheese, grated

Cook the spaghetti in a large saucepan of boiling salted water for 8–10 minutes or until tender but still firm to the bite.

Meanwhile heat the oil in a large frying pan and fry the bacon until the fat is transparent. Draw the pan off the heat. In a bowl, beat the eggs with the cream, adding a little salt and a generous grinding of pepper.

Drain the cooked spaghetti thoroughly and mix it with the bacon. Return to moderate heat for 1–2 minutes to heat through. Stir the egg mixture rapidly into the pan. As it begins to thicken, tip in the cheese. Do not stir it in. Serve immediately on hot plates.

SERVES FOUR

MRS BEETON'S TIP

Use fresh pasta with this sauce, if preferred. It will cook in considerably less time than dried pasta and will be ready as soon as it rises to the surface of the boiling water. Test after 1 minute.

Vegetarian Dishes

Whether you are vegetarian or you just love dairy foods, pulses and vegetables, here are plenty of tasty meat-free dishes.

NUT ROAST

The mixture for this delicious nut roast can be prepared ahead.

oil for frying and roasting
1 onion, finely chopped
2 cloves garlic, crushed
6 medium mushrooms, sliced
15 ml / 1 tbsp plain flour, plus extra for coating
300 ml / 10 fl oz Vegetable Stock (page 188)
175 g / 6 oz finely chopped unsalted, unroasted nuts
175 g / 6 oz breadcrumbs
1 tbsp soy or chilli sauce
2.5 ml / ½ tsp dried herbs or
30 ml / 2 tbsp fresh herbs
salt and pepper to taste

Set the oven at 190°C / 375°F / gas 5. Fry the onion over a moderate heat in about a tablespoon of oil for 5 minutes or until soft and transparent. Add the garlic and mushrooms. Cook until the mushrooms have released their juice.

Stir in the flour. Slowly pour in the stock, stirring continuously. Bring to the boil, and simmer gently for 5 minutes. Stir in the nuts, breadcrumbs, soy or chilli sauce, herbs and seasoning.

Turn the mixture on to a floured board and shape into a loaf. Heat about a tablespoon of oil in a roasting tin in the oven. Dust the loaf with flour, place in the tin and bake for 40 minutes, basting occasionally.

SERVES FOUR

FELAFEL

Serve felafel in pitta pockets, or omit the tahini and serve with Greek yogurt or Tzatziki (page 39) and salad for a simple and satisfying lunch.

200 g / 7 oz chick peas, soaked overnight or for several hours in water to cover
75 g / 3 oz fine matzo meal or wholemeal flour
5 ml / 1 tsp salt
5 ml / 1 tsp ground cumin
10ml / 2 tsp ground coriander
1 garlic clove, crushed
oil for deep frying

TAHINI
50 g / 2 oz ground sesame seeds
1 garlic clove, crushed
1.25 ml / ¼ tsp salt
15 ml / 1 tbsp lemon juice
pinch of pepper

Drain the chick peas, put them in a clean saucepan and add fresh water to cover. Bring to the boil, lower the heat and simmer for 1–1½ hours until very tender. Drain, mince the chick peas finely, or chop and sieve them.

Combine the minced chick peas, matzo meal, salt, cumin, coriander and garlic in a bowl. Form into small balls, adding 15–30 ml / 12 tbsp water if necessary.

Heat the oil to 170°C / 338°F, or until a cube of bread added to the oil browns in 1½ minutes. Add the felafel, a few at a time, and fry until golden brown. Drain them on absorbent kitchen paper; keep the felafel hot while cooking successive batches.

To make the tahini, mix all the ingredients together and add 75 ml / 5 tbsp water. Sieve to a smooth purée or process in a blender or food processor for a few minutes. Add more salt and pepper if required. Serve tahini separately.

MAKES 36

SOYA BEAN BAKE

butter or oil for greasing
450 g / 1 lb soya beans, soaked for 24 hours in cold water to cover
2 onions, finely chopped
1 green pepper, seeded and chopped
1 carrot, coarsely grated
1 celery stick, sliced
45 ml / 3 tbsp molasses
45 ml / 3 tbsp chopped parsley
5 ml / 1 tsp dried thyme
5 ml / 1 tsp dried savory or marjoram
salt and pepper
2 x 397 g / 14 oz cans chopped tomatoes
175 g / 6 oz medium oatmeal
50 g / 2 oz Lancashire or Caerphilly cheese, finely crumbled or grated
45 ml / 3 tbsp snipped chives
50 ml / 2 fl oz olive oil

Grease a large ovenproof dish – a lasagne dish is ideal. Set the oven at 180°C / 350°F / gas 4. Drain the beans. Put them in a saucepan with fresh water to cover. Bring to the boil and boil vigorously for 45 minutes. Lower the heat, add more boiling water if necessary, cover the pan and simmer for 1½–2 hours until tender. Top up the water as necessary.

Drain the beans and put them in a mixing bowl with the onions, green pepper, carrot and celery. Warm the molasses in a small saucepan and pour it over the bean mixture. Stir in the herbs and season with salt and pepper. Mix in the canned tomatoes.

Spoon the mixture into the prepared dish. Mix together the oatmeal, cheese and chives. Spoon the oatmeal mixture over the beans, then drizzle the olive oil over the top. Cover the dish with foil or a lid and bake for 45 minutes. Remove the lid and bake for a further 15 minutes. Serve hot, from the dish.

SERVES SIX

CURRIED BEANS

200 g / 7 oz dried haricot beans, soaked overnight in water to cover
30 ml / 2 tbsp oil
1 onion, finely chopped
2.5 cm / 1 inch fresh root ginger, peeled and finely chopped
2 garlic cloves, crushed
pinch of cayenne pepper
15 ml / 1 tbsp ground coriander
2.5 ml / ½ tsp turmeric
30 ml / 2 tbsp brown sugar
1 x 397 g / 14 oz can chopped tomatoes
1 bay leaf
salt and pepper
50 g / 2 oz raisins
1 eating apple, peeled, cored and diced

Drain the beans, put them in a clean saucepan and add fresh water to cover. Bring the water to the boil, boil briskly for 10 minutes, then lower the heat and simmer the beans for about 40 minutes or until just tender.

Meanwhile heat the oil in a large saucepan. Fry the onion, ginger and garlic over gentle heat for about 10 minutes. Stir in cayenne pepper to taste, with the coriander, turmeric and sugar. Fry for 5 minutes more, stirring constantly.

Drain the beans and add them, along with the canned tomatoes and bay leaf, to the onion mixture. Add salt and pepper to taste and stir well. Bring just to the boil, then lower the heat and simmer for 30 minutes. Add the raisins and apple, recover and cook gently for a further 30 minutes.

SERVES FOUR

LENTIL AND STILTON LASAGNE

This makes a delicious vegetarian main course which is full flavoured and usually enjoyed by non-vegetarians as well. Serve with a fresh, good mixture of green salad ingredients.

225 g / 8 oz green lentils
8 sheets of lasagne
salt and pepper
30 ml / 2 tbsp olive oil
1 large onion, chopped
1 garlic clove, crushed
5 ml / 1 tsp dried marjoram
225 g / 8 oz mushrooms, sliced
2 x 397 g / 14 oz cans chopped tomatoes
225 g / 8 oz ripe blue Stilton cheese (without rind)
30 ml / 2 tbsp plain flour
300 ml / ½ pint milk

Cook the lentils in plenty of boiling water for 35 minutes, until just tender. Cook the lasagne in boiling salted water with a little oil added for 12–15 minutes, or until just tender. Drain both and set the lentils aside; lay the lasagne out to dry on absorbent kitchen paper.

Heat the remaining oil in a large saucepan. Add the onion, garlic and marjoram and cook for 10 minutes, or until slightly softened. Stir in the mushrooms and cook for 5 minutes before adding the tomatoes. Stir in the cooked lentils with plenty of salt and pepper and bring to the boil. Reduce the heat and cover the pan, then simmer for 5 minutes.

Set the oven at 180°C / 350°F / gas 4. Grease a lasagne dish or large ovenproof dish. Pour half the lentil mixture into the base of the dish and top it with half the lasagne. Pour the remaining lentil mixture over the pasta, then end with the remaining pasta.

Mash the Stilton in a bowl with a sturdy fork or process it in a food processor. Sprinkle a little of the flour over the cheese and work it in, then add the remaining flour in the same way to make the mixture crumbly. Gradually work in the milk, a little at a time, pounding the cheese at first, then beating it as it softens. When the mixture is soft and creamy, the remaining milk may be incorporated more quickly. Add some pepper and just a little salt.

Pour the mixture over the lasagne, scraping the bowl clean. Bake in the preheated oven for 40–45 minutes, or until the top of the lasagne is well browned and bubbling.

SERVES SIX

VARIATION

- **Lentil and Leek Lasagne** Omit the onion in the main recipe and use 450 g / 1 lb sliced leeks. Cook them with an additional knob of butter until well reduced. Continue as above. Cheddar may be substituted for the Stilton: it should be finely grated or chopped in a food processor.

CANNELLONI WITH MUSHROOM STUFFING

butter for greasing
12–16 cannelloni
15 ml / 1 tbsp olive oil
750 ml / 1¼ pints White Sauce (page 189)
50 g / 2 oz butter
200 g / 7 oz button mushrooms, thinly sliced
50 g / 2 oz Parmesan cheese, grated
50 g / 2 oz Gruyère cheese, grated
15 ml / 1 tbsp fine dried white breadcrumbs
15 ml / 1 tbsp single cream or top of the milk

Butter a shallow ovenproof dish. Set the oven at 180°C / 350°F / gas 5. Cook the cannelloni in a saucepan of boiling salted water with the oil for 10–15 minutes until al dente. Drain well. Simmer 500 ml / 18 fl oz of the sauce until well reduced and very thick. Put the sauce on one side.

Melt 25 g / 1 oz of the butter in a pan and gently cook the mushrooms for 2 minutes. Add the mushrooms to the sauce with 25 g / 1 oz of the Parmesan. Leave to cool for 10 minutes.

Spoon the cooled mixture into the cannelloni and place in the prepared ovenproof dish. Sprinkle the Gruyère over the cannelloni, then sprinkle with the breadcrumbs. Add the cream or top of the milk to the remaining sauce and pour over the pasta. Top with the remaining Parmesan and dot with the remaining butter.

Bake for 15–20 minutes, until lightly browned. Cover with greased foil if browning too much before the end of cooking.

SERVES FOUR

RISOTTO MILANESE

75 g / 3 oz butter
30 ml / 2 tbsp olive oil
1 onion, finely chopped
350 g / 12 oz risotto rice
600 ml / 1 pint Vegetable Stock (page 188)
2.5 ml / 1 tsp saffron threads
300 ml / ½ pint dry white wine
salt and pepper
150 g / 5 oz Parmesan cheese, grated

Heat 25 g / 1 oz of the butter with the olive oil in a large saucepan. Add the onion and fry gently, stirring occasionally for 10 minutes. Add the rice and cook for a few minutes, stirring gently until all the rice grains are coated in fat. Meanwhile heat the stock to simmering point in a separate pan.

Put the saffron threads in a mortar and pound them with a pestle. Stir in a little of the hot stock to dissolve the saffron, then set aside.

Add the wine and half the remaining stock to the rice, with salt and pepper to taste. Bring to the boil. Stir once, lower the heat and cover the pan tightly. Leave over low heat for 10 minutes. Pour in half the remaining hot stock, do not stir, then cover and cook for 5 minutes, shaking the pan occasionally to prevent sticking. Finally, add the remaining stock and saffron liquid. Stir once or twice, cover and cook for about 10 minutes, until the rice is cooked, creamy and moist.

Stir in the remaining butter and the Parmesan cheese. Taste the risotto, adding more salt and pepper if required. Cover tightly and leave to stand for 5 minutes before serving.

SERVES FOUR

BLACK-EYED BEAN AND TOMATO GOULASH

225 g / 8 oz black-eyed beans, soaked in cold water overnight
1 large aubergine, trimmed and diced
salt and pepper
45 ml / 3 tbsp oil
2 large onions, chopped
1 garlic clove, crushed
4 celery sticks, diced
1 large red pepper, seeded and diced
1 bay leaf
2 fresh thyme sprigs
15 ml / 1 tbsp paprika
15 ml / 1 tbsp sugar
2 x 397 g / 14 oz cans chopped tomatoes
150 ml / ¼ pint plain yogurt

Drain the soaked beans. Put them in a saucepan with plenty of fresh water. Bring to the boil, boil vigorously for 10 minutes, then lower the heat and cover the pan. Simmer for 30–40 minutes, or until tender.

Meanwhile, place the aubergine in a colander. Sprinkle with salt, then leave over a bowl or in the sink for 30 minutes. Rinse and drain well.

Heat the oil in a saucepan. Add the chopped onion, garlic, celery, pepper, bay leaf and thyme. Cook, stirring often, for 15–20 minutes, or until the onion is soft but not brown. Add the aubergine. Cook, stirring often, for 15 minutes or until tender.

Add salt and pepper to taste, stir in the paprika and sugar, then pour in the tomatoes and bring the mixture to the boil. Drain the black-eyed beans and add them to the pan. Mix well and simmer for 5 minutes, then taste for seasoning. Top each portion with a little yogurt.

SERVES FOUR TO SIX

LENTIL AND BROCCOLI GRATIN

225 g / 8 oz green or brown lentils
2 onions, chopped
1 bay leaf
750 ml / 1¼ pints Vegetable Stock (page 188)
450 g / 1 lb broccoli, broken into small florets
30 ml / 2 tbsp oil
6 tomatoes, peeled and quartered
150 ml / ¼ pint medium cider
salt and pepper
225 g / 8 oz mozzarella cheese, diced

Place the lentils in a saucepan with 1 onion, the bay leaf and the stock. Bring to the boil, then lower the heat and cover the pan. Simmer the lentils for 40–50 minutes, until they are tender and most of the stock has been absorbed. Check that they do not become dry during cooking. Replace the cover, remove from the heat and leave to stand.

Meanwhile, cook the broccoli in a saucepan of boiling water for 2–3 minutes, until just tender. Drain. Heat the oil in a large flameproof casserole and add the remaining onion. Cook, stirring, for 10–15 minutes, or until softened. Stir in the broccoli, tomatoes and cider with salt and pepper. Cook, stirring occasionally, for 15 minutes.

Discard the bay leaf from the lentils, then tip them into the pan with the broccoli mixture. Stir to combine all the ingredients. Taste and add more salt and pepper if required. Top with the mozzarella cheese and grill until the cheese is bubbling, crisp and golden. Serve piping hot.

SERVES FOUR TO SIX

LEEK TART

8 small leeks, trimmed and washed
2 eggs
salt and pepper
grated nutmeg
25 g / 1 oz Gruyère cheese, grated

SHORT CRUST PASTRY
100 g / 4 oz plain flour
1.25 ml / ¼ tsp salt
50 g / 2 oz margarine
flour for rolling out

SAUCE
15 g / ½ oz butter
15 g / ½ oz plain flour
150 ml / ¼ pint milk, or milk and leek cooking liquid

Set the oven at 200°C / 400°F / gas 6. To make the pastry, sift the flour and salt into a bowl, then rub in the margarine until the mixture resembles fine breadcrumbs. Add enough cold water to make a stiff dough. Press the dough together with your fingertips.

Roll out the pastry on a lightly floured surface and use to line an 18-cm / 7-inch flan tin or ring placed on a baking sheet. Line the pastry with greaseproof paper and fill with baking beans. Bake 'blind' for 20 minutes, then remove the paper and beans. Return to the oven for 5 minutes, then leave to cool. Reduce the oven temperature to 190°C / 375°F / gas 5.

Using the white parts of the leeks only, tie them into two bundles with string. Bring a saucepan of salted water to the boil, add the leeks and simmer gently for 10 minutes. Drain, then squeeze as dry as possible. Cut the leeks into thick slices.

To make the sauce, melt the butter in a saucepan. Stir in the flour and cook over low heat for 2–3 minutes, without colouring. Gradually add the liquid, stirring constantly. Bring to the boil, stirring, then lower the heat and simmer for 1–2 minutes.

Beat the eggs into the white sauce. Then add salt, pepper and nutmeg to taste. Stir in half of the Gruyère. Put a layer of sauce in the cooled pastry case, cover with the leeks, then with the remaining sauce. Sprinkle with the remaining Gruyère. Bake for 20 minutes or until golden on top.

SERVES EIGHT

SPICY SPINACH AND CHICK PEAS

The use of canned chick peas makes this delicious dish a quick-cook option.

25 g / 1 oz butter
30 ml / 2 tbsp cumin seeds
15 ml / 1 tbsp coriander seeds, crushed
15 ml / 1 tbsp mustard seeds
1 large onion, chopped
2 garlic cloves, crushed
2 x 425 g / 15 oz cans chick peas, drained
5 ml / 1 tsp turmeric
1 kg / 2¼ lb fresh spinach, cooked
salt and pepper

Melt the butter in a saucepan, add the cumin, coriander and mustard seeds and cook gently, stirring, for about 3 minutes, or until the seeds are aromatic. Keep the heat low to avoid burning the butter.

Add the onion and garlic to the pan and continue to cook for about 15 minutes, until the onion is softened. Stir in the chick peas and turmeric and cook for 5 minutes, until thoroughly hot. Tip the spinach into the pan and stir it over moderate heat until heated through. Season and serve.

SERVES FOUR TO SIX

LENTIL PASTIES

100 g / 4 oz split red lentils
300 ml / ½ pint Vegetable Stock (page 188)
25 g / 1 oz butter
salt and pepper
pinch of grated nutmeg
4 button mushrooms, sliced
15 ml / 1 tbsp double cream
beaten egg or milk for glazing

SHORT CRUST PASTRY
225 g / 8 oz plain flour
2.5 ml / ½ tsp salt
100 g / 4 oz margarine
flour for rolling out

Make the pastry. Sift the flour and salt into a bowl, then rub in the margarine until the mixture resembles fine breadcrumbs. Add enough cold water to make a stiff dough. Press the dough together with your fingertips. Wrap in greaseproof paper and chill until required.

Put the lentils in a saucepan with the vegetable stock. Bring to the boil, lower the heat and cover the pan. Simmer for 20 minutes or until the lentils are soft and all the liquid is absorbed. Beat in the butter and season with salt, pepper and nutmeg. Stir in the mushrooms and cream and set aside. Set the oven at 200°C / 400°F / gas 6.

Roll out the pastry very thinly on a floured surface, and cut into eight 13-cm / 5-inch rounds. Divide the lentil filling between the rounds, dampen the edges and fold over to form ½ circles. Press the edges together and seal firmly, then brush with a little beaten egg or milk. Place on baking sheets and bake for about 15 minutes, or until the pastry is cooked and browned.

MAKES EIGHT

SWISS CHEESE FONDUE

Cheese fondue is traditionally made in an open ceramic or earthenware pan called a caquelon. *The pan is set on a spirit lamp or burner, which can be regulated to prevent the cheese mixture from burning. Long-handled fondue forks enable each guest to spear a cube of bread and dip it into the fondue mixture. The golden crust which forms in the bottom of the pan is a traditional, end-of-fondue treat.*

1 garlic clove
300 ml / ½ pint light dry white wine
350 g / 12 oz Emmental cheese, grated
450 g / 1 lb Gruyère cheese, grated
10 ml / 2 tsp cornflour or potato flour
15 ml / 1 tbsp kirsch
white pepper and grated nutmeg
2 long French sticks, cubed

Cut the garlic clove in half; rub the cut sides over the inside of a fondue pan or flameproof casserole. Pour the wine into the pan or casserole and heat until steaming, but not simmering. Gradually add the grated cheese, a little at a time, stirring constantly. Allow each addition of cheese to melt before adding the next. Remove the pan from the heat.

Mix the cornflour or potato flour to a paste with the kirsch and stir this into the fondue. Return to the heat and cook, stirring constantly, until the mixture is smooth, thick and creamy. Add pepper and nutmeg to taste. Set the pan over a burner or hotplate at the table. Serve at once, with the bread.

SERVES SIX TO EIGHT

MRS BEETON'S TIP

Don't drink anything cold with this fondue or the cheese will re-solidify in your stomach and be hard to digest.

TOFU PARCELS

butter for greasing
1 carrot, diced
100 g / 4 oz fine French beans, thinly sliced
salt and pepper
2 spring onions, chopped
30 ml / 2 tbsp chopped parsley
4 large sheets of filo pastry
50 g / 2 oz butter, melted, or 60 ml / 4 tbsp olive oil
100 g / 4 oz low-fat soft cheese
with garlic and herbs
275 g / 10 oz smoked tofu, quartered

WATERCRESS CREAM
1 bunch of watercress, trimmed and chopped
5 ml / 1 tsp grated lemon rind
150 ml / ¼ pint soured cream, fromage frais or
Greek-style yogurt

Blanch the carrot and French beans in a saucepan of boiling salted water for 2 minutes, then drain and mix with the spring onions and parsley. Set the oven at 200°C / 400°F / gas 6. Grease a baking sheet.

Work on 1 sheet of filo at a time, keeping the others covered. Brush the pastry with butter or olive oil and fold it in half. Place a quarter of the soft cheese in the middle, spreading it slightly but taking care not to tear the pastry. Divide the vegetable mixture into quarters. Use a teaspoon to sprinkle half of one portion over the cheese.

Top with a quarter of the tofu, diced, then sprinkle the remainder of the vegetable portion over.

Fold one side of the filo over the filling, brush lightly with butter or oil, then fold the opposite side over, pressing the pastry together. Brush with more fat and fold the two remaining sides over as before to make a neat parcel. Brush the top with a little oil or butter, then invert the parcel on the prepared baking sheet, so that the thicker layers of pastry are underneath. Brush the top with more fat. Repeat with the remaining pastry and filling.

Bake the parcels for about 30 minutes, until golden and crisp. Meanwhile, mix the watercress, lemon rind and soured cream, fromage frais or yogurt in a bowl. Add a little salt and pepper. Use a metal slice to transfer the parcels to serving plates and serve at once, with the watercress cream.

SERVES FOUR

MRS BEETON'S TIP

Instead of making individual parcels, use the same filling ingredients to make a pie. Increase the number of filo pastry sheets to line a flan dish, overlapping them and ensuring the pastry is at least two layers thick. Dice the tofu and spread it out with the rest of the filling. Top with more filo, then fold over the excess from lining the dish. Bake at 180°C / 350°F / gas 4 for about 45 minutes, to allow the filo base to cook through.

USING TOFU

- Marinate chunks with olive oil, garlic and marjoram, then coat with tomato sauce, top with grated cheese and bake.
- Combine with leeks, mushrooms, courgettes and walnuts or cheese, and use as a filling for pastries and pies.
- Smoked tofu makes a tasty salad ingredient.
- Purée tofu with a little milk to make a creamy sauce, then pour over a layer of cooked vegetables and bake until golden.
- Marinate firm tofu in soy sauce, garlic, sesame oil and sherry. Stir fry gently with shredded vegetables, adding the marinade to make a sauce.
- Marinate firm tofu with herbs and oil or with a Chinese-style mixture as above. Coat with egg and breadcrumbs or flour and deep fry or bake until crisp and golden. Serve with a crisp green salad.

TOFU AND SPRING ONION STIR FRY

This tasty stir fry goes well with cooked rice or Oriental noodles.

350 g / 12 oz firm tofu cut into 2.5-cm / 1-inch cubes
1 garlic clove, crushed
45 ml / 3 tbsp soy sauce
5 cm / 2 inch fresh root ginger, peeled and chopped
5 ml / 1 tsp sesame oil
5 ml / 1 tsp cornflour
30 ml / 2 tbsp dry sherry
60 ml / 4 tbsp Vegetable Stock (page 188)
30 ml / 2 tbsp oil
1 red pepper, seeded and diced
1 bunch of spring onions, trimmed and sliced diagonally
100 g / 4 oz button mushrooms, sliced
salt and pepper

Place the tofu in a large, shallow dish. Mix the garlic, soy sauce, ginger and sesame oil in a bowl, then sprinkle the mixture evenly over the tofu. Cover and leave to marinate for 1 hour. In a jug, blend the cornflour to a paste with the sherry, then stir in the stock and set aside.

Heat the oil in a wok or large frying pan. Add the tofu and stir fry until lightly browned. Add the pepper and continue cooking for 2–3 minutes before stirring in the spring onions. Once the onions are combined with the tofu, make a space in the middle of the pan and stir fry the mushrooms for 2 minutes. Pour in the cornflour mixture and stir all the ingredients together. Bring the juices to the boil, stirring all the time, then lower the heat and simmer for 2 minutes. Taste the mixture for seasoning, then serve.

SERVES FOUR

EGGS FLORENTINE

butter for greasing
1 kg / 2¼ lb fresh spinach or
2 x 225 g / 8 oz packets frozen leaf spinach
15 ml / 1 tbsp butter
salt and pepper
4 eggs
100 g / 4 oz Fontina or Cheddar cheese,
finely grated

Set the oven at 190°C / 375°F / gas 5. Wash the fresh spinach several times and remove any coarse stalks. Put into a saucepan with just the water that clings to the leaves, then cover the pan with a tight-fitting lid. Place over moderate heat for about 3 minutes, shaking the pan often until the spinach has wilted. Lower the heat slightly and cook for 3–5 minutes more. (Cook frozen spinach according to the directions on the packet.)

When the spinach is tender, drain it thoroughly in a colander. Cut through the leaves several times with a knife to chop them roughly. Melt the butter in the clean pan, add the spinach with salt and pepper to taste, and heat through gently.

Spoon into a greased ovenproof dish and, using the back of a spoon, make 4 small hollows in the surface. Break an egg into each hollow, add salt and pepper to taste, then sprinkle the grated cheese over the eggs. Bake for 12–15 minutes until the eggs are lightly set. Serve at once.

SERVES FOUR

OMELETTE

The secret of a light omelette is to add water, not milk, to the mixture, beating it only sufficiently to mix the yolks and whites. The mixture must be cooked quickly until evenly and lightly set, then served when still moist. Have everything ready before you start to cook, including the diner, so that the omelette can be taken to the table as soon as it is ready.

2 eggs
salt and pepper
15 ml / 1 tbsp butter

Break the eggs into a bowl, add 15 ml / 1 tbsp cold water, salt and pepper. Beat lightly with a fork. Thoroughly heat a frying pan or omelette pan. When it is hot, add the butter , tilting the pan so that the whole surface is lightly greased. Without drawing the pan off the heat, add the egg mixture. Leave to stand for 10 seconds.

Using a spatula, gently draw the egg mixture from the sides to the centre as it sets, allowing the uncooked egg to run in to fill the gap. Do not stir or the mixture will scramble.

When the omelette is golden and set underneath, but still slightly moist on top, remove it from the heat. Loosen the edges by shaking the pan, using a round-bladed knife or the edge of a spatula, then flip one-third of the omelette towards the centre. Flip the opposite third over towards the centre. Tip the omelette onto a hot plate, folded sides underneath. Alternatively, the cooked omelette may be rolled out of the pan after the first folding, so that it is served folded in three. A simpler method is to fold the omelette in half in the pan, then slide it out on to the plate.

SERVES ONE

FILLINGS

- **Cheese** Add 40 g / 1½ oz grated cheese to the beaten eggs. Sprinkle a further 15 g / ½ oz over the omelette.
- **Fines Herbes** Add 2.5 ml / ½ tsp chopped fresh tarragon, 2.5 ml / ½ tsp chopped fresh chervil, 5 ml / 1 tsp chopped parsley and a few snipped chives to the beaten eggs.
- **Mushroom** Fry 50 g / 2 oz sliced mushrooms in butter. Spoon into the centre of the omelette just before folding.

MRS BEETON'S TIP

In Mrs Beeton's day, most households would have had a special cast-iron omelette pan. When new, this would be 'seasoned' by melting a little butter in the pan, sprinkling it with salt, and rubbing vigorously with a soft cloth. This process helped to prevent the egg mixture from sticking. The omelette pan would not be washed after use; instead it would be rubbed all over with a soft cloth. Salt would be used, if necessary, to remove any egg still sticking to the pan.

SPANISH OMELETTE

Known as tortilla, a Spanish omelette is quite different from filled and folded omelettes or featherlight soufflé omelettes. It is a thick cake of potato and onion set in eggs, cut into wedges and served hot or cold. This classic potato omelette is quite delicious without any additional ingredients; however, the recipe is often varied to include red and green peppers or a mixture of vegetables, such as peas and green beans.

675 g / 1½ lb potatoes
225 g / 8 oz onions, thinly sliced
salt and pepper
45 ml / 3 tbsp olive oil
6 eggs, beaten

Cut the potatoes into 1-cm / ½-inch cubes and mix them with the onions in a basin. Add plenty of seasoning and mix well.

Heat the oil in a heavy-bottomed frying pan which has fairly deep sides. Add the potatoes and onions, then cook, stirring and turning the vegetables often, until both potatoes and onions are tender. This takes about 25 minutes.

Pour the eggs over the potatoes and cook over medium heat, stirring, until the eggs begin to set. Press the vegetables down evenly and leave to set. Lower the heat to prevent the base of the omelette overbrowning before the eggs have set sufficiently.

Lay a large plate over the omelette and invert the pan to turn the omelette out on the plate. The base of the pan should be well greased but if it looks a little dry, then add a little extra olive oil and heat it. Slide the omelette back into the pan and cook over medium to high heat for 3–5 minutes, until crisp and browned. Serve the omelette hot, warm or cold.

SERVES FOUR TO SIX

Side Dishes

Rice, pasta and a whole array of potato dishes feature alongside other tasty accompaniments to enhance your main course and introduce variety and colour to your table.

COOKING RICE

225 g / 8 oz long-grain rice
salt and pepper

If using Basmati rice, plain, untreated long-grain rice or wild rice, start by placing the grains in a bowl. Wash the rice in several changes of cold water, taking care not to swirl the grains vigorously as this may damage them. Pour off most of the water each time, then add fresh water and swirl the rice gently with your fingertips. Finally drain the rice in a sieve and turn it into a saucepan.

Add cold water: 600 ml / 1 pint for white rice; 750 ml / 1¼ pints for brown or wild rice. Add a little salt and bring to the boil. Stir once, then lower the heat and put a tight-fitting lid on the pan. Cook very gently until the grains are tender: 15–20 minutes for easy-cook varieties and white rice; usually 20 minutes for Basmati rice; 25–35 minutes for brown rice; 40–50 minutes for wild rice.

Remove the pan from the heat and leave, covered, for 5 minutes, then fork up the grains, add salt and pepper if liked, and serve the rice.

SERVES FOUR

VARIATIONS

- **Saffron Rice** Add 3 green cardamom pods and a bay leaf to the rice. Reduce the amount of water by 50 ml / 2 fl oz. Pound 2.5–5 ml / ½–1 tsp saffron strands to a powder in a mortar with a pestle. Add 50 ml / 2 fl oz boiling water and stir well until the saffron has dissolved. Sprinkle this over the rice after it has been cooking for 15 minutes, then replace the lid quickly and finish cooking. Fork up the rice before serving, removing the bay leaf and cardomom pods.
- **Pilau Rice** Cook 1 chopped onion in a little butter or ghee in a large saucepan, then add 1 cinnamon stick, 1 bay leaf, 4 green cardomoms and 4 cloves. Stir in 225 g / 8 oz Basmati rice and 600 ml / 1 pint water and cook as in the main recipe. In a separate pan, cook a second onion, this time thinly sliced, in 50 g / 2 oz butter or ghee until golden brown. Add 30 ml / 2 tbsp cumin seeds (preferably black seeds) when the onion has softened and

before it begins to brown. Add half the sliced onion mixture to the rice and fork it in. Pour the remaining onion mixture over the top of the rice before serving. Saffron may be added to pilau, or for a colourful mixture, mix in ⅓ saffron rice to ⅔ pilau rice as above.

- **Brown and Wild Rice** Mix different grains for an interesting texture. Start by cooking the wild rice for 10 minutes, then add the brown rice and continue cooking until the brown rice is tender.
- **Walnut Rice** Cook the chosen rice; add 100 g / 4 oz chopped walnuts and 30 ml / 2 tbsp chopped parsley before serving.
- **Lemon Rice** Add the grated rind of 1 lemon to the rice: if it is added at the beginning of cooking it gives a deep-seated flavour; added just before serving it adds a fresh, zesty tang to the rice.
- **Rice with Herbs** Add bay leaves, sprigs of rosemary, thyme, savory or sage to the rice at the beginning of cooking. Alternatively, sprinkle chopped parsley, fresh tarragon, dill, mint or marjoram over the rice at the end of cooking. Match the herb to the flavouring in the main dish, with which the rice is to be served.
- **Tomato Rice** Add 1 finely chopped onion, 1 bay leaf and 30 ml / 2 tbsp tomato purée to the rice before cooking.

RICE MOULDS

A rice mould may be large or small and it may be served hot or cold. Making a rice ring is the popular form of moulding rice so that the middle may be filled with a hot sauced mixture or cold dressed salad. Typical fillings are salmon, tuna, or mixed seafood in a white sauce, or chicken in sauce. Salads of seafood or poultry, dressed with mayonnaise, soured cream or fromage frais, turn a rice ring into a rich main dish; light vegetable mixtures, such as tomato or courgette salad, are ideal for moulds which are intended as a side dish.

For best results, and particularly when making large moulds, avoid easy-cook rice and mixtures with a high proportion of wild rice as the grains tend not to cling together well. The basic recipe opposite or any of the flavoured variations may be used to make the moulds and rings that follow.

- **Hot Ring Mould** Cook 1 quantity of the rice. Set the oven at 180°C / 350°F / gas 4. Meanwhile, thoroughly grease a 1.1-litre / 2-pint metal ring mould with either butter or oil. Stir 45 ml / 3 tbsp single cream or milk into the rice, then press it into the mould and cover the top with foil. Bake for 30 minutes. Turn out on a warmed serving dish.
- **Cold Rice Ring** Cook 1 quantity of rice. Grease a 1.1-litre / 2-pint ring mould with oil. Press the cooked rice into it, cover and cool. Chill lightly before inverting the mould on a serving dish.
- **Individual Moulds** These may be either hot or cold, using tins or individual ovenproof basins for hot moulds. Grease the moulds well, using oil for cold rice. Dariole moulds, individual basins and ramekin dishes are all ideal. Follow the instructions for ring moulds, reducing the cooking time to 20 minutes for a hot mould.
- **Multi-layered Moulds** With contrasting layers which are visually pleasing, the shape of the mould can be extremely simple, such as a plain round tin or soufflé dish. Combine two or three layers, remembering that the layer in the base of the dish will be on top when the rice is unmoulded. For example, begin by placing a layer of Lemon Rice in the mould, then add a layer of Tomato Rice and finally add a layer of Rice with Herbs, mixing in plenty of chopped parsley after cooking. This combination is excellent with plain grills, such as barbecued foods.

PASTA

SAUCES FOR PASTA

Sauces are the natural partners for pasta, whether you choose a plain tomato or rich meat sauce to serve Italian style; or toss a succulent, sauced stir fry with Chinese egg noodles to produce a tempting chow mein.

Seafood, poultry and meat sauces take pasta beyond the realms of snack and supper cookery to dinner-party status. Meat-free dishes are quickly conjured up by combining buttery braised vegetable mixtures with fresh cooked pasta.

PASTA SIMPLICITY

One of the most appealing aspects of pasta cookery is that it can be ultra simple, extremely stylish and absolutely mouthwatering. One classic Italian dish is piping hot pasta, generously dressed with olive oil in which a few crushed cloves of garlic have been lightly cooked. Sprinkled with some shredded basil or chopped parsley, topped with several grindings of black pepper and a few spoonfuls of freshly grated Parmesan cheese, this is indeed a snack to set before the hungriest gourmet.

USES FOR PASTA

- **Serving with Sauce** Shapes, noodles, spaghetti, Chinese egg noodles.
- **Layering and Baking or Grilling** Lasagne, medium-sized shapes, cut macaroni.
- **Filling** Fresh pasta dough, cannelloni, large shells, large elbow shapes or other large shapes with a pocket or hollow for stuffing.
- **Soups** Very small shapes, cut macaroni, vermicelli, Oriental rice noodles.
- **As a Stuffing** For filling scooped out tomatoes and other vegetables such as peppers, soup pasta, macaroni and small shapes are all suitable.

Pasta recipes can be found in this book on pages 76, 131, 132, 133, 134, 140, 141 and 142.

SCALLOPED POTATOES WITH ONIONS

butter for greasing
675 g / 1½ lb potatoes, peeled and cut into 5-mm / ¼-inch slices
450 g / 1 lb onions, sliced in rings
salt and pepper
125 ml / 4 fl oz milk or cream
20 ml / 4 tsp butter

Grease a baking dish. Set the oven at 190°C / 375°F / gas 5. Layer the potatoes and onions in the prepared dish, sprinkling salt and pepper between the layers and ending with potatoes. Pour the milk or cream over the top. Dot the surface with butter and cover with foil or a lid.

Bake for 1½ hours, removing the cover for the last 20–30 minutes of the cooking time to allow the potatoes on the top to brown.

SERVES FOUR TO SIX

DUCHESSE POTATOES

butter or margarine for greasing
450 g / 1 lb old potatoes
salt and pepper
25 g / 1 oz butter or margarine
1 egg or 2 egg yolks
grated nutmeg (optional)
beaten egg for brushing

Grease a baking sheet. Cut the potatoes into pieces and cook in a saucepan of salted water for 15–20 minutes. Drain thoroughly, then press the potatoes through a sieve into a large mixing bowl.

Set the oven at 200°C / 400°F / gas 6. Beat the butter or margarine and egg or egg yolks into the potatoes. Add salt and pepper to taste and the nutmeg, if used. Spoon the mixture into a piping bag fitted with a large rose nozzle. Pipe rounds of potato on to the prepared baking sheet. Brush with a little beaten egg. Bake for about 15 minutes, until golden brown.

SERVES SIX

POTATOES SAVOYARDE

1 small garlic clove, cut in half
75 g / 3 oz Gruyère cheese, grated
1 kg / 2¼ lb potatoes, thinly sliced
salt and pepper
freshly grated nutmeg
40 g / 1½ oz butter
about 375 ml / 13 fl oz Chicken Stock (page 187)
or Vegetable Stock (page 188)

Set the oven at 190°C / 375°F / gas 5. Rub the cut garlic all over the inside of a 2-litre / 3½-pint baking dish. Set aside 30 ml / 2 tbsp of the grated cheese.

Put the potatoes into a mixing bowl. Add salt, pepper and a little nutmeg to taste, then mix in the remaining cheese. Use a little of the butter to grease the baking dish generously, add the potato mixture and pour in just enough stock to cover the potatoes. Dot the remaining butter over the potatoes and sprinkle with the reserved grated cheese. Bake for 1¼ hours or until golden brown and the potatoes are tender.

SERVES SIX

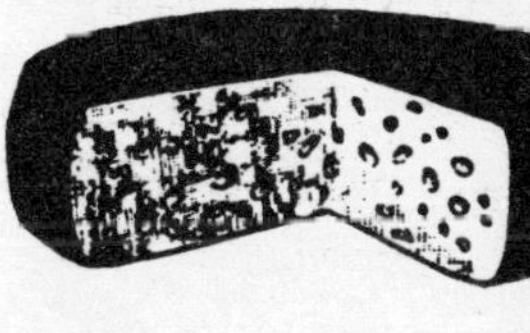

GRATIN DAUPHINOIS

25 g / 1 oz butter
1 kg / 2¼ lb, potatoes, thinly sliced
1 large onion, about 200 g / 7 oz, thinly sliced
200 g / 7 oz Gruyère cheese, grated
salt and pepper
grated nutmeg
125 ml / 4 fl oz single cream

Butter a 1.5-litre / 2¾-pint casserole, reserving the remaining butter. Set the oven at 190°C / 375°F / gas 5. Bring a saucepan of water to the boil, add the potatoes and onion, then blanch for 30 seconds. Drain.

Put a layer of potatoes in the bottom of the prepared casserole. Dot with a little of the butter, then sprinkle with some of the onion and cheese, a little salt, pepper and grated nutmeg. Pour over some of the cream. Repeat the layers until all the ingredients have been used, finishing with a layer of cheese. Pour the remaining cream on top.

Cover and bake for 1 hour. Remove from the oven and place under a hot grill for 5 minutes, until the top of the cheese is golden brown and bubbling.

SERVES SIX

ANNA POTATOES

butter for greasing
1 kg / 2¼ lb even-sized potatoes
salt and pepper
melted clarified butter (see Mrs Beeton's Tip)

Grease a 20-cm / 8-inch round cake tin and line the base with greased greaseproof paper. Set the oven at 190°C / 375°F / gas 5.

Trim the potatoes so that they will give equal-sized slices. Slice them very thinly using either a sharp knife or a mandoline. Arrange a layer of potatoes, slightly overlapping, in the base of the tin. Add salt and pepper to taste, then spoon a little clarified butter over them. Make a second layer of potatoes and spoon some more butter over them. Complete these layers until all the potatoes have been used. Cover the tin with greased greaseproof paper and foil.

Bake for 1 hour. Check the potatoes several times during cooking and add a little more clarified butter if they become too dry. Invert the tin on to a warm serving dish to remove the potatoes. Serve at once.

SERVES SIX

MRS BEETON'S TIP

To clarify butter, heat gently until melted, then stand for 2–3 minutes. Pour off the clear yellow liquid on top and allow to solidify. This is the clarified butter.

BAKED JACKET POTATOES

4 large, even-sized baking potatoes
oil for brushing (optional)
butter or flavoured butter, to serve

Set the oven at 200°C / 400°F / gas 6. Scrub the potatoes, dry them with absorbent kitchen paper and pierce the skin several times with a skewer. If you like soft jackets, brush the potatoes all over with oil.

Bake the potatoes directly on the oven shelf for 1–1½ hours. Test by pressing gently with the fingers. To serve, cut a cross in the top of each potato with a sharp knife. Squeeze the sides of the potato so that the top opens up. Add a pat of plain or flavoured butter and serve.

SERVES FOUR

MICROWAVE TIP

Cooking jacket potatoes in the microwave has practically become a national pastime. Prick the potatoes several times with a skewer or they may burst. Cook directly on the microwave rack or wrap in absorbent kitchen paper if a very soft potato is preferred. For crisper potatoes, brush with oil or butter after microwave cooking, then crisp under a hot grill, turning once. Jacket potatoes also cook extremely well in a combination microwave oven. Follow the instructions in your handbook.

MICROWAVE COOKING TIMES ON HIGH (600–650 watt ovens)
Large potatoes (350 g / 12 oz): *1 potato – 8 minutes; 2 potatoes – 15 minutes; 4 potatoes – 27 minutes*
Medium potatoes (150 g / 5 oz): *1 potato – 4 minutes; 2 potatoes – 5–6 minutes; 4 potatoes – 10 minutes; 6 potatoes – 18–19 minutes*

FILLINGS

Make a meal of baked jacket potatoes by cutting them in half, scooping out the centres and mashing them with selected ingredients. Pile the fillings back into the potato shells and heat through, if necessary, in a 180°C / 350°F / gas 4 oven for about 20 minutes. Alternatively, reheat in the microwave oven or under a moderate grill.

- **Cheese and Ham** Mash the potato. Grate in 100 g / 4 oz Cheddar cheese, add 50 g / 2 oz chopped ham (use trimmings for economy) and mix with 25 g / 1 oz softened butter. Replace in oven until golden.
- **Kipper** Mash the potato with 75 g / 3 oz flaked cooked kipper. Add 1 chopped hard-boiled egg, with salt and pepper to taste. Thin with a little milk, if necessary. Reheat.
- **Frankfurter** Mash the potato with butter. For each potato, add 2 heated chopped frankfurters, 15 ml / 1 tbsp tomato relish and chopped parsley.

TOPPINGS

The easy option. Cut the potatoes almost but not quite in half and open out. Top with any of the mixtures suggested below.

- **Blue Cheese and Yogurt** Mash 100 g / 4 oz ripe Danish blue cheese. Mix with 150 ml / ¼ pint Greek yogurt.
- **Sausage and Chutney** Mix hot or cold sliced cooked sausage with diced eating apple, chopped spring onions and a little of your favourite chutney.
- **Egg Mayonnaise** Mash hard-boiled eggs with a little mayonnaise or plain yogurt. Add 5 ml / 1 tsp tomato ketchup or tomato purée and snipped chives.
- **Sardine** Mash canned sardines in tomato sauce and mix with diced cucumber. Serve with shredded lettuce.
- **Chick pea** Mash 100 g / 4 oz drained canned chick peas and mix with 1 crushed garlic clove and 15–30 ml / 1–2 tbsp Greek yogurt. Top with chopped spring onion and sesame seeds.
- **Cheese Soufflé** Combine 100 g / 4 oz grated Cheddar cheese and 1 beaten egg. Cut potatoes in half, pile some of the mixture on each half and grill until topping puffs up and turns golden brown.
- **Peas and Bacon** Combine 100 g / 4 oz cooked petits pois and 3 crumbled grilled rindless bacon rashers. Top with a knob of butter.
- **Broccoli and Asparagus** Mix 175 g / 6 oz cooked broccoli and 100 g / 4 oz drained canned asparagus tips. Stir in 150 ml / ¼ pint soured cream and season with salt and pepper to taste.
- **Southern Special** Warm 100–150 g / 4–5 oz creamed sweetcorn. Spoon on to potatoes. Top each portion with 2 grilled rindless bacon rashers and 3–4 banana slices.

MRS BEETON'S POTATO RISSOLES

Mrs Beeton suggests that these rissoles may be made very simply, without the onion, or that their flavour may be improved by adding a little chopped cooked tongue or ham.

50 g / 2 oz butter
1 large onion, finely chopped
350 g / 12 oz hot mashed potato
salt and pepper
10 ml / 2 tsp chopped parsley
2 eggs, beaten
75 g / 3 oz dried white breadcrumbs
oil for shallow frying

Melt half the butter in a frying pan. Cook the onion, stirring often, until soft but not browned. Season the mashed potato generously, then stir in the parsley and onion with all the butter from the pan. Allow the mixture to cool completely. When cold, shape the mixture into small balls.

Put the beaten egg in a shallow bowl and spread the breadcrumbs on a plate or sheet of foil. Dip the potato rissoles in the egg, then coat them thoroughly in breadcrumbs. Place them on a baking sheet and chill for 15 minutes to firm the mixture.

Heat the remaining butter with the oil for shallow frying in a deep frying pan. Put in the rissoles and turn them in the hot fat for 6–9 minutes until golden brown all over. Drain on absorbent kitchen paper and serve hot.

MAKES ABOUT TEN

GLAZED ONIONS

Glazed onions make a tasty accompaniment to grilled steak, baked ham or bacon chops. They are often used as a garnish.

400 g / 14 oz button onions
Chicken Stock (page 187) (see method)
salt and pepper
15 ml / 1 tbsp soft light brown sugar
25 g / 1 oz butter
pinch of grated nutmeg

Skin the onions and put them in a single layer in a large saucepan. Add just enough stock to cover. Bring to a simmering point and cook for 15–20 minutes until the onions are just tender, adding a small amount of extra stock if necessary.

By the time the onions are cooked, the stock should have reduced almost to a glaze. Remove from the heat and stir in the remaining ingredients. Turn the onions over with a spoon so that the added ingredients mix well and the onions are coated in the mixture.

Return the pan to the heat until the onions become golden and glazed. Serve at once, with the remaining syrupy glaze.

SERVES FOUR

VARIATION

- **Citrus Glazed Onions** Melt 25 g / 1 oz butter in a frying pan. Add 400 g / 14 oz button onions. Sprinkle with 15 ml / 1 tbsp soft light brown sugar. Add salt and pepper to taste and fry, turning the onions occasionally until golden brown. Stir in 150 ml / ¼ pint orange juice and 10 ml / 2 tsp lemon juice. Cover and simmer for 15 minutes.

CARROTS WITH CIDER

This traditional way of cooking carrots was originally known as the 'conservation method' because it preserved as many of the nutrients as possible.

75 g / 3 oz butter
675 g / 1½ lb young carrots, trimmed and scraped
salt
60 ml / 4 tbsp double cream
125 ml / 4 fl oz dry cider
few drops of lemon juice
pepper

Melt 25 g / 1 oz of the butter in a heavy-bottomed saucepan. Add the carrots and cook over very gentle heat for 10 minutes, shaking the pan frequently so that the carrots do not stick to the base. Pour over 100 ml / 3½ fl oz boiling water, with salt to taste. Cover the pan and simmer the carrots for about 10 minutes more or until tender. Drain, reserving the liquid for use in soup or stock.

Melt the remaining butter in the clean pan. Gradually stir in the cream and cider. Add the lemon juice and salt and pepper to taste. Stir in the carrots, cover the pan and cook gently for 10 minutes more. Serve at once.

SERVES SIX

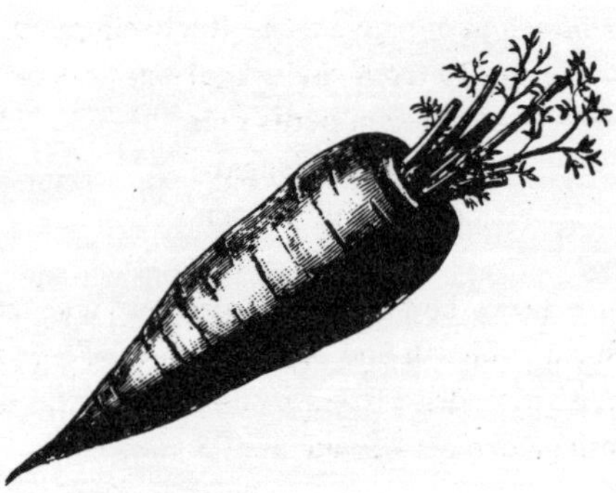

GLAZED CARROTS

50 g / 2 oz butter
575 g / 1¼ lb young carrots, scraped but left whole
3 sugar cubes, crushed
1.25 ml / ¼ tsp salt beef stock (see method)
15 ml / 1 tbsp chopped parsley to garnish

Melt the butter in a saucepan. Add the carrots, sugar and salt. Pour in enough stock to half cover the carrots. Cook over gentle heat, without covering the pan, for 15–20 minutes or until the carrots are tender. Shake the pan occasionally to prevent sticking.

Using a slotted spoon, transfer the carrots to a bowl and keep hot. Boil the stock rapidly in the pan until it is reduced to a rich glaze. Return the carrots to the pan, two or three at a time, turning them in the glaze until thoroughly coated. Place on a heated serving dish, garnish with parsley and serve at once.

SERVES SIX

PETITS POIS À LA FRANÇAISE

50 g / 2 oz butter
1 lettuce heart, shredded
1 bunch of spring onions, finely chopped
675 g / 1½ lb fresh shelled garden peas or frozen petits pois
pinch of sugar
salt and pepper

Melt the butter in a heavy-bottomed saucepan and add the lettuce, spring onions, peas and sugar, with salt and pepper to taste. Cover and simmer very gently until the peas are tender. Frozen petits pois may be ready in less than 10 minutes, but fresh garden peas could take 25 minutes.

SERVES SIX

COURGETTES WITH ALMONDS

The cooked courgettes should be firm and full flavoured, not overcooked and watery.

25 g / 1 oz butter
25 g / 1 oz blanched almonds, split in half
450 g / 1 lb courgettes, trimmed and thinly sliced
salt and pepper
30 ml / 2 tbsp snipped chives or chopped parsley

Melt the butter in a large frying pan. Add the almonds and fry over moderate heat, stirring, until lightly browned. Tip the courgettes into the pan and cook, regularly turning the slices until golden.

Tip the courgettes into a heated serving dish, add salt and pepper to taste and sprinkle the chives or parsley over them. Serve at once.

SERVES FOUR TO SIX

BEANS WITH SOURED CREAM

butter for greasing
450 g / 1 lb runner beans
150 ml / ¼ pint soured cream
1.25 ml / ¼ tsp grated nutmeg
1.25 ml / ¼ tsp caraway seeds
salt and pepper
50 g / 2 oz butter
50 g / 2 oz fresh white breadcrumbs

Set the oven at 200°C / 400°F / gas 6. Grease a 1-litre / 1¾-pint baking dish. Wash the beans, string them if necessary and slice them thinly. Cook in boiling water for 3–7 minutes until cooked to taste. Alternatively, cook in a steamer over boiling water. Drain thoroughly.

Combine the soured cream, nutmeg and caraway seeds in a bowl. Stir in salt and pepper to taste. Add the beans and toss well together. Spoon the mixture into the baking dish.

Melt the butter in a small frying pan, add the breadcrumbs and fry over gentle heat for 2–3 minutes. Sprinkle the mixture over the beans. Bake in the preheated oven for 20–30 minutes or until the topping is crisp and golden.

SERVES THREE TO FOUR

BUTTERED LEEKS

50 g / 2 oz butter
675 g / 1½ lb leeks, trimmed, sliced and washed
15 ml / 1 tbsp lemon juice
salt and pepper
30 ml / 2 tbsp single cream (optional)

Melt the butter in a heavy-bottomed saucepan. Add the leeks and lemon juice, with salt and pepper to taste. Cover the pan and cook the leeks over very gentle heat for about 30 minutes or until very tender. Shake the pan from time to time to prevent the leeks from sticking to the base. Serve in the cooking liquid. Stir in the cream when serving, if liked.

SERVES FOUR

MRS BEETON'S TIP

Leeks can be very gritty. The easiest way to wash them is to trim the roots and tough green leaves, slit them lengthways to the centre, and hold them open under cold running water to flush out the grit.

CAULIFLOWER CHEESE

salt and pepper
1 firm cauliflower
30 ml / 2 tbsp butter
60 ml / 4 tbsp plain flour
200 ml / 7 fl oz milk
125 g / 4½ oz Cheddar cheese, grated
pinch of dry mustard
pinch of cayenne pepper
25 g / 1 oz dried white breadcrumbs

Bring a saucepan of salted water to the boil, add the cauliflower, cover the pan and cook gently for 20–30 minutes until tender. Drain well, reserving 175 ml / 6 fl oz of the cooking water. Leave the cauliflower head whole or cut carefully into florets. Place in a warmed ovenproof dish, cover with greased greaseproof paper and keep hot.

Set the oven at 220°C / 425°F / gas 7, or preheat the grill. Melt the butter in a saucepan, stir in the flour and cook for 1 minute. Gradually add the milk and reserved cooking water, stirring all the time until the sauce boils and thickens. Remove from the heat and stir in 100 g / 4 oz of the cheese, stirring until it melts into the sauce. Add the mustard and cayenne and season with salt and pepper to taste.

Pour the sauce over the cauliflower. Mix the remaining cheese with the breadcrumbs and sprinkle them on top. Brown the topping for 7–10 minutes in the oven or under the grill. Serve at once.

SERVES FOUR

VARIATIONS

- A wide variety of vegetables can be cooked in this way. Try broccoli (particularly good with grilled bacon); small whole onions; celery, celeriac; leeks or chicory (both taste delicious if wrapped in ham before being covered in the cheese sauce) and asparagus. A mixed vegetable gratin – cooked sliced carrots, green beans, onions and potatoes – also works well. Vary the cheese topping too: Red Leicester has good flavour and colour; Gruyère or Emmental is tasty with leeks or chicory; a little blue cheese mixed with the Cheddar will enliven celery or celeriac.

CAULIFLOWER POLONAISE

1 large cauliflower, trimmed
salt
50 g / 2 oz butter
50 g / 2 oz fresh white breadcrumbs
2 hard-boiled eggs
15 ml / 1 tbsp chopped parsley

Put the cauliflower, stem down, in a saucepan. Pour over boiling water, add salt to taste and cook for 10–15 minutes or until the stalk is just tender. Drain the cauliflower thoroughly in a colander.

Meanwhile, melt the butter in a frying pan, add the breadcrumbs and fry until crisp and golden.

Chop the egg whites finely. Sieve the yolks and mix them with the parsley in a small bowl.

Drain the cauliflower thoroughly and place it on a heated serving dish. Sprinkle first with the breadcrumbs and then with the egg yolk mixture. Arrange the chopped egg white around the edge of the dish. Serve at once.

SERVES FOUR

GARLANDED ASPARAGUS

30 asparagus spears
75 g / 3 oz butter
salt and pepper
50 g / 2 oz Parmesan cheese, grated
4 egg yolks, unbroken
butter for frying

Set the oven at 200°C / 400°F / gas 6. Prepare and cook the asparagus (see page 24). Drain thoroughly and place in an ovenproof dish. Melt half the butter in a small frying pan and spoon it over the top. Sprinkle with salt and pepper to taste and top with the Parmesan. Bake for 15 minutes or until the topping is golden brown.

Meanwhile, add the remaining butter to the frying pan and melt over gentle heat. Add the egg yolks, taking care not to break them, and cook gently until just set outside, basting often. Using an egg slice, carefully lift them out of the pan, draining off excess fat, and arrange them around the asparagus. Serve at once.

SERVES FOUR

MUSHROOMS IN CREAM SAUCE

50 g / 2 oz butter
450 g / 1 lb small button mushrooms
10 ml / 2 tsp arrowroot
125 ml / 4 fl oz Chicken Stock (page 187)
or Vegetable Stock (page 188)
15 ml / 1 tbsp lemon juice
30 ml / 2 tbsp double cream
salt and pepper
30 ml / 2 tbsp chopped parsley

Melt the butter in large frying pan, add the mushrooms and fry over gentle heat without browning for 10 minutes.

Put the arrowroot in a small bowl. Stir in 30 ml / 2 tbsp of the stock until smooth. Add the remaining stock to the mushrooms and bring to the boil. Lower the heat and simmer gently for 15 minutes, stirring occasionally. Stir in the arrowroot, bring to the boil, stirring, then remove the pan from the heat.

Stir in the lemon juice and cream, with salt and pepper to taste. Serve sprinkled with parsley.

SERVES FOUR TO SIX

RED CABBAGE WITH APPLES

This dish improves in flavour if made 1–2 days in advance.

45 ml / 3 tbsp oil
1 onion, finely chopped
1 garlic clove, crushed
900 g / 2 lb red cabbage, finely shredded
2 large cooking apples
15 ml / 1 tbsp soft light brown sugar or golden syrup
juice of ½ lemon
30 ml / 2 tbsp red wine vinegar
salt and pepper
15 ml / 1 tbsp caraway seeds (optional)

Heat the oil in a large saucepan, add the onion and garlic and fry gently for 5 minutes. Add the cabbage. Peel, core and slice the apples and add them to the pan with the sugar or syrup. Cook over very gentle heat for 10 minutes, shaking the pan frequently.

Add the lemon juice and vinegar, with salt and pepper to taste. Stir in the caraway seeds, if used. Cover and simmer gently for 1–1½ hours, stirring occasionally and adding a little water if the mixture appears dry. Check the seasoning before serving.

SERVES SIX

RATATOUILLE

Traditionally, the vegetable mixture is cooked gently for about 45–60 minutes and it is richer, and more intensely flavoured if prepared ahead, cooled and thoroughly reheated. This recipe suggests cooking for slightly less time, so that the courgettes and aubergines still retain a bit of bite; the final simmering time may be shortened, if liked, to give a mixture in which the courgettes contribute a slightly crunchy texture.

2 aubergines
salt and pepper
125–150 ml / 4–5 fl oz olive oil
2 large onions, finely chopped
2 garlic cloves, crushed
2 peppers, seeded and cut into thin strips
30 ml / 2 tbsp chopped fresh marjoram or
10 ml / 2 tsp dried marjoram
450 g / 1 lb tomatoes, peeled and chopped
4 courgettes, thinly sliced
30 ml / 2 tbsp finely chopped parsley or mint

Cut the ends off the aubergines and cut them into cubes. Put the cubes in a colander and sprinkle generously with salt. Set aside for 30 minutes, then rinse thoroughly, drain and pat dry on absorbent kitchen paper.

Heat some of the oil in a large saucepan or flameproof casserole, add some of the aubergine cubes and cook over moderate heat, stirring frequently, for 10 minutes. Using a slotted spoon, transfer the aubergine to a bowl; repeat until all the cubes are cooked, adding more oil as necessary. Add the onions to the oil remaining in the pan and fry for 5 minutes, until slightly softened. Stir in the garlic, peppers and marjoram, with salt and pepper to taste. Cook, stirring occasionally for 15–20 minutes, or until the onions are thoroughly softened.

Add the tomatoes and courgettes to the mixture. Replace the aubergines, heat until bubbling, then cover and simmer for a further 15–20 minutes, stirring occasionally. Serve hot, sprinkled with parsley, or cold, sprinkled with mint.

SERVES FOUR TO SIX

Sauces, Stocks & Stuffings

These recipes transform everyday dishes into gourmet treats.

CHESTNUT AND ONION STUFFING

Use double the quantity listed below when stuffing the neck end of a 5–6 kg / 11–13 lb turkey.

1 large onion, thickly sliced
125 ml / 4 fl oz Chicken Stock (page 187) or water
450 g / 1 lb chestnuts, prepared and cooked (see Mrs Beeton's Tip) or 300 g / 11 oz canned chestnuts
salt and pepper
1 egg, beaten

Combine the onion and stock or water in a small saucepan. Bring the liquid to the boil, lower the heat and simmer for about 10 minutes until the onion is tender, drain and chop finely.

Meanwhile mince the chestnuts or chop them finely. Combine the chestnuts and onion in a bowl, stir in salt and pepper to taste and add enough of the beaten egg to bind the stuffing.

SUFFICIENT FOR 1 x 2.5 kg / 5½ lb DUCK

MRS BEETON'S TIP

To prepare chestnuts, make a slit in the rounded side of each nut, then bake them in a preheated 180°C / 350°F / gas 4 oven for 30 minutes or cook them in boiling water for 20 minutes. Remove the shells and skins while still hot. Put the shelled nuts in a saucepan with just enough stock to cover. Bring the liquid to the boil, lower the heat and simmer for 45–60 minutes or until the nuts are tender.

LEMON AND HERB STUFFING

50 g / 2 oz butter
100 g / 4 oz fresh white breadcrumbs
30 ml / 2 tbsp chopped parsley
2.5 ml / ½ tsp chopped fresh thyme
grated rind of ½ lemon
salt and pepper

Melt the butter in a small saucepan. Add the breadcrumbs, herbs and lemon rind. Add salt and pepper to taste, then use as required.

SUFFICIENT FOR 8 x 75 g / 3 oz THIN FISH FILLETS

SAGE AND ONION STUFFING

2 onions, thickly sliced
4 young fresh sage sprigs or
10 ml / 2 tsp dried sage
100 g / 4 oz fresh white breadcrumbs
50 g / 2 oz butter or margarine, melted
salt and pepper
1 egg, lightly beaten (optional)

Put the onions in a small saucepan with water to cover. Bring to the boil, cook for 2–3 minutes, then remove the onions from the pan with a slotted spoon. Chop them finely. Chop the sage leaves finely, discarding any stalk.

Combine the breadcrumbs, onions and sage in a bowl. Add the melted butter or margarine and season with salt and pepper to taste. Mix well. If the stuffing is to be shaped into balls, bind it with the beaten egg.

SUFFICIENT FOR 1 x 2.5 kg / 5½ lb DUCK;
DOUBLE THE QUANTITY FOR 1 x 4–5 kg / 9–11 lb GOOSE

APPLE AND CELERY STUFFING

3 rindless streaky bacon rashers, chopped
1 onion, finely chopped
1 celery stick, finely sliced
3 large cooking apples
75 g / 3 oz fresh white breadcrumbs
15 ml / 1 tbsp grated lemon rind
salt and pepper

Heat the bacon gently in a frying pan until the fat runs, then increase the heat and fry until browned, stirring frequently. Using a slotted spoon, transfer the bacon to a bowl. Add the onion and celery to the fat remaining in the frying pan and fry over moderate heat for 5 minutes. Remove with a slotted spoon, add to the bacon and mix lightly.

Peel, core and dice the apples. Add them to the pan and fry until soft and lightly browned. Add to the bacon mixture with the breadcrumbs and lemon rind. Mix well, adding salt and pepper to taste.

SUFFICIENT FOR 1 x 4–5 kg / 9–11 lb GOOSE, 2 x 2.5 kg / 5½ lb DUCKS OR 1 BONED PORK JOINT

MRS BEETON'S TIP

Many delicatessens and deli counters in supermarkets sell packets of bacon bits – the trimmings left after slicing. These are ideal for a recipe such as this, and may also be used in quiches, on pizzas and to flavour soups and stews.

MRS BEETON'S FORCEMEAT

100 g / 4 oz gammon or rindless bacon, finely chopped
50 g / 2 oz shredded beef suet
grated rind of 1 lemon
5 ml / 1 tsp chopped parsley
5 ml / 1 tsp chopped mixed herbs
salt
cayenne pepper
pinch of ground mace
150 g / 5 oz fresh white breadcrumbs
2 eggs, lightly beaten

Combine the gammon or bacon, suet, lemon rind and herbs in a bowl. Add salt, cayenne and mace to taste. Mix well with a fork, then stir in the breadcrumbs. Gradually add enough beaten egg to bind.

MAKES ABOUT 350 g / 12 oz

VARIATION

- **Mrs Beeton's Forcemeat Balls** Roll the mixture into 6–8 small balls. Either cook the forcemeat balls around a roast joint or bird, or fry them in a little oil until browned and cooked through.

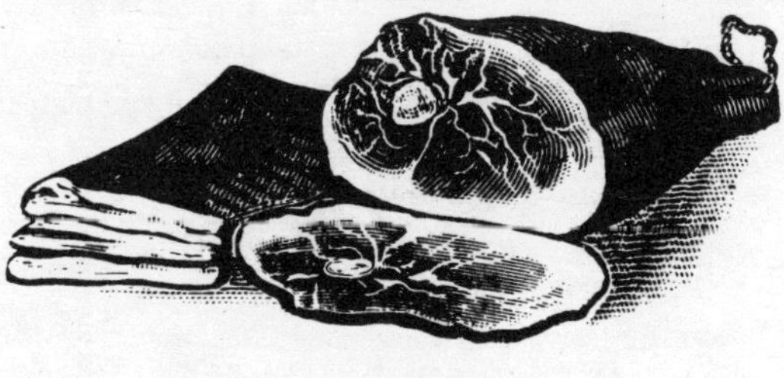

GRAVY

giblets, carcass bones or trimmings from meat, poultry or game
1 bay leaf
1 thyme sprig
1 clove
6 black peppercorns
1 onion, sliced
pan juices from roasting (see Mrs Beeton's Tip)
25 g / 1 oz plain flour (optional)
salt and pepper

Place the giblets, bones, carcass and/or trimmings (for example wing ends) in a saucepan. Pour in water to cover, then add the bay leaf, thyme, clove, peppercorns and onion. Bring to the boil and skim off any scum, then lower the heat, cover the pan and simmer for about 1 hour.

Strain the stock and measure it. You need about 600–750 ml / 1–1¼ pints to make gravy for up to six servings. If necessary, pour the stock back into the saucepan and boil until reduced.

Pour off most of the fat from the roasting tin, leaving a thin layer and all the cooking juices. Place the tin over moderate heat; add the flour if the gravy is to be thickened. Cook the flour, stirring all the time and scraping all the sediment off the tin, for about 3 minutes, until it is browned. If the gravy is not thickened, pour in about 300 ml / ½ pint of the stock and boil, stirring and scraping, until the sediment on the base of the tin is incorporated.

Slowly pour in the stock (or the remaining stock, if making thin gravy), stirring all the time. Bring to the boil and cook for 2–3 minutes to reduce the gravy and concentrate the flavour slightly. Taste and add more salt and pepper if required.

SERVES FOUR TO SIX

MRS BEETON'S TIP

The quality of the sediment on the base of the cooking tin determines the quality of the gravy. If the meat was well seasoned and roasted until well browned outside, the sediment should have a good colour and flavour. Any herbs (other than large stalks), onions or flavouring roasted under the meat should be left in the pan until the gravy is boiled, then strained out before serving.

GRAVY NOTES

- If making gravy for a meal other than a roast, for example to accompany sausages or toad-in-the-hole, use a little fat instead of the pan juices and brown the flour well over low to moderate heat. Meat dripping gives the best flavour but butter or other fat may be used.
- To make onion gravy, slowly brown 2 thinly sliced onions in the fat before adding the flour – this is excellent with grilled sausages or toad-in-the-hole.
- Gravy browning may be added if necessary; however, it can make the sauce look artificial and unpleasant. Pale gravy is perfectly acceptable, provided it has good flavour.
- Always taste gravy when cooked. It should be well seasoned. If it lacks flavour, or is rather dull, a dash of Worcestershire sauce, mushroom ketchup or about 5–15 ml / 1–3 tsp tomato purée may be whisked in.
- Gravy may be enriched by adding up to half wine instead of stock.
- Add 60 ml / 4 tbsp port or sherry, and 15 ml / 1 tbsp redcurrant jelly to make a rich gravy for duck, game, lamb, pork or venison.
- Add 2 chopped pickled walnuts and 15 ml / 1 tbsp walnut oil to the pan juices to make a delicious walnut gravy.
- Use vegetable stock to make vegetable gravy. Cook a finely diced carrot and 2 thinly sliced onions in butter or margarine instead of using meat juices. Add 1.25 ml / ¼ tsp ground mace and 30 ml / 2 tbsp chopped parsley.
- Add 100 g / 4 oz thinly sliced mushrooms to the pan juices to make a mushroom gravy. The sauce may be further enriched by adding a little mushroom ketchup.

FISH STOCK

fish bones and trimmings without gills, which cause bitterness
5 ml / 1 tsp salt
1 small onion, sliced
2 celery sticks, sliced
4 white peppercorns
1 bouquet garni

Break up any bones and wash the fish trimmings, if used. Put the bones, trimmings or heads in a saucepan and cover with 1 litre / 1¾ pints cold water. Add the salt.

Bring the liquid to the boil and add the vegetables, peppercorns and bouquet garni. Lower the heat, cover and simmer gently for 30–40 minutes. Do not cook the stock for longer than 40 minutes or it may develop a bitter taste. Strain, cool quickly and use as required.

MAKES ABOUT 1 litre / 1¾ pints

COURT BOUILLON

This is the traditional cooking liquid for poached fish and is discarded after use.

500 ml / 17 fl oz dry white wine or dry cider
30 ml / 2 tbsp white wine vinegar
2 large carrots, sliced
2 large onions, sliced
2–3 celery sticks, chopped
6 parsley stalks. crushed
1 bouquet garni
10 peppercorns, lightly crushed
salt and pepper

Pour the wine or cider into a large stainless steel or enamel saucepan. Add 1 litre / 1¾ pints water along with the remaining ingredients. Bring to the boil, lower the heat and simmer for 30 minutes. Cool, then strain and use as required.

MAKES 1.5 litres / 2¾ pints

VARIATION

- **White Wine Fish Stock** Add 100 ml / 3½ fl oz dry white wine, 4–5 mushroom stalks and 1 sliced carrot. Simmer for 30 minutes only.

CHICKEN STOCK

4 chicken drumsticks or 1 meaty chicken carcass
1 small onion, sliced
1 carrot, roughly chopped
1 celery stick, sliced
1 bouquet garni
5 ml / 1 tsp white peppercorns

Break or chop the carcass into manageable pieces. Put it in a large saucepan with 1.75 litres / 3 pints cold water. Bring to the boil; skim the surface. Add the remaining ingredients, lower the heat and simmer for 3–4 hours. Cool quickly, then strain. Skim off surface fat. Season and use as required.

MAKES ABOUT 1.4 litres / 2½ pints

VARIATION

- **Rich Chicken Stock** Use drumsticks and roast them at 200°C / 400°F / gas 6 for 40 minutes. Drain off the fat. Continue as above, adding 225 g / 8 oz cubed belly pork with the chicken.
- **Game Stock** Use the carcasses of 1 or 2 game birds such as pheasant or grouse, with the giblets, instead of the chicken.

VEGETABLE STOCK

Vary the vegetables according to the market selection and your personal taste.

2 onions, sliced
2 leeks, trimmed, sliced and washed
1 small turnip, chopped
4 celery sticks, sliced
2 tomatoes, chopped
1 bouquet garni
6 black peppercorns
2 cloves
a few lettuce leaves
a few spinach leaves
a few watercress sprigs
2.5 ml / ½ tsp yeast extract (optional)
salt

Put the root vegetables, celery, tomatoes, herbs and spices in a large saucepan. Pour in 2 litres / 3½ pints water. Bring to the boil, lower the heat and simmer for 1 hour.

Add the lettuce, spinach and watercress and simmer for 1 hour more. Stir in the yeast extract, if using, and add salt to taste.

MAKES ABOUT 1.75 litres / 3 pints

WHITE SAUCE

The recipe that follows is for a thick coating sauce.

50 g / 2 oz butter
50 g / 2 oz plain flour
600 ml / 1 pint milk, stock or a mixture
salt and pepper

Melt the butter in a saucepan. Stir in the flour and cook over low heat for 2–3 minutes, without browning.

With the heat on the lowest setting, gradually add the liquid, stirring constantly. If lumps begin to form, stop pouring in liquid and stir the sauce vigorously, then continue pouring in the liquid when smooth. Increase the heat to moderate and cook the sauce, stirring, until it boils and thickens.

Lower the heat and simmer for 1–2 minutes, beating briskly to give the sauce a gloss. Add salt and pepper to taste.

MAKES 600 ml / 1 pint

VARIATION

- **Pouring Sauce** Follow the recipe above, but use only 40 g / 1½ oz each of butter and flour.
- **Cheese Sauce** Add 100 g / 4 oz grated cheese.

MRS BEETON'S TIP

White Sauce can be made by the all-in-one method. Simply combine the butter, flour and liquid in a saucepan and whisk over moderate heat until the mixture comes to the boil. Lower the heat and simmer for 3–4 minutes, whisking constantly until the sauce is thick, smooth and glossy. Add salt and pepper to taste.

HOLLANDAISE SAUCE

This is the classic sauce to serve with asparagus, poached salmon or other firm fish.

45 ml / 3 tbsp white wine vinegar
6 peppercorns
bay leaf
1 blade of mace
3 egg yolks
100 g / 4 oz butter, softened
salt and pepper

Combine the vinegar, peppercorns, bay leaf and mace in a small saucepan. Boil rapidly until the liquid is reduced to 15 ml / 1 tbsp. Strain into a heatproof bowl and leave to cool.

Add the egg yolks and a nut of butter to the vinegar and place over a pan of gently simmering water. Heat the mixture gently, beating constantly until thick. Do not allow it to approach boiling point.

Add the remaining butter, a little at a time beating well after each addition. When all the butter has been added the sauce should be thick and glossy.

MICROWAVE TIP

A quick and easy Hollandaise Sauce can be made in the microwave oven. Combine 30 ml / 2 tbsp lemon juice with 15 ml / 1 tbsp water in a large bowl. Add a little salt and white pepper and cook on High for 3–6 minutes or until the mixture is reduced by about two-thirds. Meanwhile place 100 g / 4 oz butter in a measuring jug. Remove the bowl of lemon juice from the microwave oven, replacing it with the jug of butter. Heat the butter on High for 2½ minutes. Meanwhile add 2 large egg yolks to the lemon juice, whisking constantly. When the butter is hot, add it in the same way. Return the sauce to the microwave oven. Cook on High for 30 seconds, whisk once more and serve.

If the sauce curdles, whisk in 10 ml / 2 tsp cold water. If this fails to bind it, put an egg yolk in a clean bowl and beat in the sauce gradually. Add a little salt and pepper and serve the sauce lukewarm.

MAKES ABOUT 125 ml / 4 fl oz

BÉARNAISE SAUCE

The classic accompaniment to grilled beef steak, Béarnaise Sauce is also delicious with vegetables such as broccoli.

60 ml / 4 tbsp white wine vinegar
15 ml / 1 tbsp chopped shallot
5 black peppercorns, lightly crushed
1 bay leaf
2 fresh tarragon stalks, chopped, or
1.25 ml / ¼ tsp dried tarragon
1.25 ml / ¼ tsp dried thyme
2 egg yolks
100 g / 4 oz butter, cut into small pieces
salt and pepper

Combine the vinegar, chopped shallot, peppercorns and herbs in a small saucepan. Boil until the liquid is reduced to 15 ml / 1 tbsp, then strain into a heatproof bowl. Cool, then stir in the egg yolks.

Place the bowl over a saucepan of simmering water and whisk until the eggs start to thicken. Gradually add the butter, whisking after each addition, until the sauce is thick and creamy. Add salt and pepper to taste.

MAKES ABOUT 175 ml / 6 fl oz

BÉCHAMEL SAUCE

Marquis Louis de Béchameil is credited with inventing this French foundation sauce. For a slightly less rich version, use half white stock and half milk.

1 small onion, thickly sliced
1 small carrot, sliced
1 small celery stick, sliced
600 ml / 1 pint milk
1 bay leaf
few parsley stalks
1 fresh thyme sprig
1 clove
6 white peppercorns
1 blade of mace
salt
50 g / 2 oz butter
50 g / 2 oz plain flour
60 ml / 4 tbsp single cream (optional)

Combine the onion, carrot, celery and milk in a saucepan. Add the herbs and spices, with salt to taste. Heat to simmering point, cover, turn off the heat and allow to stand for 30 minutes to infuse, then strain.

Melt the butter in a saucepan. Stir in the flour and cook over low heat for 2–3 minutes, without browning. With the heat on the lowest setting, gradually add the flavoured milk, stirring constantly.

Increase the heat to moderate, stirring until the mixture boils and thickens to a coating consistency. Lower the heat when the mixture boils and simmer the sauce for 1–2 minutes, beating briskly to give the sauce a gloss. Stir in the cream, if used, and remove the sauce from the heat at once. Do not allow the sauce to come to the boil again. Add salt if required.

MAKES ABOUT 600 ml / 1 pint

FRESH TOMATO SAUCE

Fresh tomato sauce has a multitude of uses in savoury cookery. It is one of the simplest accompaniments for plain cooked pasta, it is included in many baked dishes and it is, of course, excellent with grilled fish, poultry and meat.

30 ml / 2 tbsp olive oil
1 onion, finely chopped
1 garlic clove, crushed
1 bay leaf
1 rindless streaky bacon rasher, chopped
800 g / 1¾ lb tomatoes, peeled and chopped
60 ml / 4 tbsp stock or red wine
salt and pepper
generous pinch of sugar
15 ml / 1 tbsp chopped fresh basil or
5 ml / 1 tsp dried basil

Heat the oil in a saucepan and fry the onion, garlic, bay leaf and bacon over gentle heat for 15 minutes.

Stir in the remaining ingredients except the basil. Heat until bubbling, then cover the pan and simmer gently for 30 minutes or until the tomatoes are reduced to a pulp.

Rub the sauce through a sieve into a clean saucepan or purée in a blender or food processor until smooth, then rub it through a sieve to remove seeds, if required. Reheat the sauce. Add the basil. Add more salt and pepper if required before serving.

MAKES ABOUT 600 ml / 1 pint

BARBECUE SAUCE

This is a very adaptable sauce.
It can be used as a marinade, as a basting sauce
for chicken portions, steaks, chops and similar foods
being cooked on the barbecue grill, or as a
side sauce to serve with grilled meats.

30 ml / 2 tbsp oil
1 onion, finely chopped
2 garlic cloves, crushed
1 x 397 g / 14 oz can chopped tomatoes
45 ml / 3 tbsp red wine vinegar
30 ml / 2 tbsp soft dark brown sugar
30 ml / 2 tbsp tomato ketchup
10 ml / 2 tsp soy sauce
10 ml / 2 tsp Worcestershire sauce
salt and pepper

Heat the oil in a saucepan. Add the onion and garlic and fry over gentle heat for 4–6 minutes, until the onion is soft but not coloured. Stir in the remaining ingredients and bring to the boil. Lower the heat and simmer for 30–45 minutes, until the sauce is thick and well flavoured.

MAKES ABOUT 150 ml / ¼ pint

CREAMY MUSHROOM SAUCE

50 g / 2 oz butter
175 g / 6 oz button mushrooms, sliced
25 g / 1 oz plain flour
300 ml / ½ pint milk
75 g / 3 oz full fat soft cheese, cubed
salt and pepper
5–10 ml / 1–2 tsp lemon juice (optional)

Melt 25 g / 1 oz of the butter in a small saucepan. Add the mushrooms and fry over very gentle heat for 10 minutes until soft but not browned.

In a second saucepan, melt the remaining butter. Stir in the flour and cook for 1–2 minutes. Gradually add the milk, stirring constantly until the mixture boils and thickens.

Remove the pan from the heat and beat in the cheese, a few cubes at a time. Fold in the mushrooms, with the pan juices, and add salt and pepper to taste. Stir in the lemon juice, if using, and reheat the sauce gently without boiling. Serve in a sauceboat.

MAKES ABOUT 350 ml / 12 fl oz

TARTARE SAUCE

2 hard-boiled egg yolks
2 egg yolks
salt and pepper
15 ml / 1 tbsp white wine vinegar
300 ml / ½ pint oil (olive oil or a mixture of olive with grapeseed or sunflower oil)
15 ml / 1 tbsp chopped capers
15 ml / 1 tbsp chopped gherkin
30 ml / 2 tbsp chopped parsley
15 ml / 1 tbsp snipped chives

Sieve the hard-boiled egg yolks into a bowl. Add one of the raw yolks and mix thoroughly, then work in the second raw yolk. Stir in salt and pepper to taste and mix to a paste with the vinegar.

Beating vigorously, gradually add the oil, drop by drop, as for making Mayonnaise (page 197). When all the oil has been incorporated, and the mixture is thick, stir in the capers, gherkin and herbs.

MAKES ABOUT 300 ml / ½ pint

PESTO GENOVESE

*A little pesto goes a long way to flavour pasta.
Put the pasta in a heated serving bowl or individual dishes,
add the pesto and toss lightly. Serve at once.*

2 garlic cloves, roughly chopped
25–40 g / 1–1½ oz fresh basil leaves, roughly chopped
25 g / 1 oz pine nuts, chopped
40 g / 1½ oz Parmesan cheese, grated
juice of 1 lemon
salt and pepper
75–100 ml / 3–3½ fl oz olive oil

Combine the garlic, chopped basil leaves, pine nuts, Parmesan, lemon juice, salt and pepper in a mortar. Pound with a pestle until smooth. Alternatively, process in a blender or food processor. While blending, trickle in the oil as when making Mayonnaise (page 197), until the sauce forms a very thick paste.

SERVES FOUR

MRS BEETON'S TIP

Basil has a particular affinity with Italian dishes and it is worth growing it in a large pot on the patio during summer. For a simple starter with a wonderful taste, try sliced tomatoes topped with mozzarella cheese, a drizzle of olive oil and chopped fresh basil leaves.

MAYONNAISE

Buy eggs from a reputable supplier and make sure they are perfectly fresh. Immediately before using, wash the eggs in cold water and dry them on absorbent kitchen paper.

2 egg yolks
salt and pepper
5 ml / 1 tsp caster sugar
5 ml / 1 tsp Dijon mustard
about 30 ml / 2 tbsp lemon juice
250 ml / 8 fl oz oil (olive oil or a mixture of olive and grapeseed or sunflower oil)

Place the egg yolks in a medium bowl. Add salt and pepper, sugar, mustard and 15 ml / 1 tbsp of the lemon juice. Whisk thoroughly until the sugar has dissolved. An electric whisk is best; or use a wire whisk and work vigorously. Whisking all the time, add the oil drop by drop so that it forms an emulsion with the egg yolks. As the oil is incorporated, and the mixture begins to turn pale, it may be added in a slow trickle. If the oil is added too quickly before it begins to combine with the eggs, the sauce will curdle.

The mayonnaise may be made in a blender or food processor. The egg mixture should be processed first, with 10 ml / 2 tsp of the oil added right at the beginning. With the machine running, add the rest of the oil drop by drop at first, then in a trickle as above.

When all the oil has been incorporated the mayonnaise should be thick and pale. Taste the mixture, then stir in more lemon juice, salt and pepper, if necessary. Keep mayonnaise in a covered container in the refrigerator for up to 5 days.

MAKES ABOUT 300 ml / ½ pint

VARIATION

- **Aïoli** (good with fresh vegetable crudités) Add 2 fresh large crushed garlic cloves to the yolks with the seasonings.
- **Rouille** (good in soups) Add 2 fresh large crushed garlic cloves to the yolks. Omit the mustard. Add 15 ml / 1 tbsp paprika and 1.25 ml / ¼ tsp cayenne pepper to the yolk mixture before incorporating the oil.

APPLE SAUCE

450 g / 1 lb apples
4 cloves
15 g / ½ oz butter
rind and juice of ½ lemon
sugar (see method)

Peel, core and slice the apples. Put them in a saucepan with 30 ml / 2 tbsp water, add the cloves, butter and lemon rind. Cover and cook over low heat until the apple is reduced to a pulp. Remove the cloves. Beat until smooth, rub through a sieve or process in a blender or food processor. Return the sauce to the clean pan, stir in the lemon juice and add sugar to taste. Reheat gently, stirring until the sugar has dissolved. Serve hot or cold.

MAKES ABOUT 350 ml / 12 fl oz

HORSERADISH SAUCE

60 ml / 4 tbsp grated horseradish
5 ml / 1 tsp caster sugar
5 ml / 1 tsp salt
2.5 ml / ½ tsp pepper
10 ml / 2 tsp prepared mustard
malt vinegar (see method)
45–60 ml / 3–4 tbsp single cream (optional)

Mix the horseradish, sugar, salt, pepper and mustard in a non-metallic bowl. Stir in enough vinegar to make a sauce with the consistency of cream. The flavour and appearance will be improved if the quantity of vinegar is reduced, and the single cream added.

MAKES ABOUT 150 ml / ¼ pint

Desserts

Desserts are all the more important when entertaining guests. From the lightest sorbets and water ices to indulgent chocolate, caramel and cream desserts, round off your meal with a home-made treat. This chapter also includes advice on planning a cheese course.

MANDARIN WATER ICE

50 g / 2 oz lump sugar
6 mandarins
225 g / 8 oz caster sugar
3.75ml / ¾ tsp liquid glucose
2 lemons
2 oranges

Turn the freezing compartment or freezer to the coldest setting about 1 hour before making the water ice.

Rub the sugar lumps over the rind of the mandarins to extract some of the zest. Put the sugar lumps in a heavy-bottomed saucepan with the caster sugar and 300 ml / ½ pint water.

Dissolve the sugar over gentle heat without stirring. Bring the mixture to the boil and boil gently for about 10 minutes or until the mixture registers 110°C / 225°F on a sugar thermometer. Remove the scum as it rises in the pan.

Strain the syrup into a large bowl and stir in the liquid glucose. Pare the rind very thinly from 1 lemon and 1 orange and add to the bowl of syrup. Cover and set aside to cool.

Squeeze all the fruit and add the juice to the cold syrup mixture. Strain through a nylon sieve into a suitable container. Cover the container closely and freeze until half-frozen (when ice crystals appear around the edge of the mixture). Beat the mixture thoroughly, scraping off any crystals. Replace the cover and freeze until solid. Return the freezer to the normal setting.

Transfer the water ice to the refrigerator about 15 minutes before serving, to allow it to soften and 'ripen'. Serve in scoops in individual dishes or glasses.

SERVES SIX TO EIGHT

BOMBE TORTONI

This is absurdly easy to make, yet it makes an impressive finale for a dinner party.

300 ml / ½ pint double cream
150 ml / ¼ pint single cream
50 g / 2 oz icing sugar, sifted
2.5 ml / 1 tsp vanilla essence
2 egg whites
100 g / 4 oz hazelnut biscuits or ratafias, crushed
30 ml / 2 tbsp sherry

Turn the freezing compartment or freezer to the coldest setting about 1 hour before making the bombe. Lightly oil a 1.25-litre / 2¼-pint bombe mould or pudding basin.

Combine the creams in a large bowl and whip until thick, adding half the icing sugar. Add the vanilla essence.

In a clean, grease-free bowl whisk the egg whites until stiff. Fold in the remaining icing sugar.

Lightly fold the meringue mixture into the whipped cream. Stir in the hazelnut biscuits and sherry. Spoon the mixture into the prepared mould.

Put the lid on the bombe mould or cover the basin with foil. Freeze until firm, then return the freezer to the normal setting. To turn out, dip the mould or basin in cold water, and invert on to a chilled serving dish. Transfer to the refrigerator 15 minutes before serving to allow the ice cream to soften and 'ripen'.

SERVES SIX TO EIGHT

VARIATIONS

- Try crushed ginger biscuits with coffee liqueur instead of sherry, or crumbled meringue with cherry brandy.

SUMMER PUDDING

This delectable dessert started life with the cumbersome name of Hydropathic Pudding. It was originally invented for spa patients who were forbidden rich creams and pastries. Vary the fruit filling if you wish – blackberries or bilberries make very good additions – but keep the total quantity of fruit at about 1 kg / 2¼ lb.

150 g / 5 oz caster sugar
225 g / 8 oz blackcurrants or redcurrants, stalks removed
225 g / 8 oz ripe red plums, halved and stoned
1 strip of lemon rind
225 g / 8 oz strawberries, hulled
225 g / 8 oz raspberries, hulled
8–10 slices of day-old white bread, crusts removed

Put the sugar into a saucepan with 60 ml / 4 tbsp water. Heat gently, stirring, until the sugar has dissolved. Add the black- or redcurrants, plums and lemon rind and poach until tender.

Add the strawberries and raspberries to the saucepan and cook for 2 minutes. Remove from the heat and, using a slotted spoon, remove the lemon rind.

Cut a circle from 1 slice of bread to fit the base of a 1.25-litre / 2¼-pint pudding basin. Line the base and sides of the basin with bread, leaving no spaces. Pour in the stewed fruit, reserving about 45–60 ml / 3–4 tbsp of the juice in a jug. Top the stewed fruit filling with more bread slices. Cover with a plate or saucer that exactly fits inside the basin. Put a weight on top to press the pudding down firmly. Leave in a cool place for 5–8 hours, preferably overnight.

Turn out carefully on to a plate or shallow dish to serve. If there are any places on the bread shell where the juice from the fruit filling has not penetrated, drizzle a little of the reserved fruit juice over. Serve with whipped cream or plain yogurt.

SERVES SIX

FREEZER TIP

After the pudding has been weighted, pack the basin in a polythene bag, seal and freeze for up to 3 months. Thaw overnight in the refrigerator. Alternatively, line the basin completely with cling film before making the pudding. Thicker microwave cooking film is stronger than ordinary film, or use a double layer. Leave plenty of film overhanging the rim of the basin. Freeze the weighted pudding, then use the film to remove it from the basin. Pack and label before storing.

MRS BEETON'S ORANGE SALAD

5 oranges
50 g / 2 oz caster sugar (or to taste)
2.5 ml / ½ tsp ground mixed spice
100 g / 4 oz muscatel raisins
60 ml / 4 tbsp brandy

Peel four oranges, removing all pith. Slice them, discarding the pips. Mix the sugar and spice in a bowl. Layer the orange slices in a serving dish, sprinkling each layer with the sugar mixture and raisins.

Squeeze the juice from the remaining orange and sprinkle it over the salad. Pour over the brandy, cover and leave to macerate for 24 hours before serving.

SERVES FOUR

GREEN FRUIT SALAD

A fruit salad, fresh, crisp and flavoursome, is the perfect ending for a meal. Using shades of a single colour can be most effective. Here the theme is green and white, but golden or red colours can look equally attractive. There is no need to stick to the selection or the proportions of fruit in the recipe; simply remember that you will need a total of about 1 kg / 2¼ lb. The fruit is traditionally served in syrup but fresh fruit juices, sometimes spiked with alcohol, are equally popular today.

175 g / 6 oz green-fleshed melon, scooped into balls
175 g / 6 oz seedless green grapes
2 Granny Smith apples
2 kiwi fruit, peeled and sliced
2 greengages, halved and stoned
2 passion fruit
mint sprigs to decorate

SYRUP
175 g / 6 oz sugar
30 ml / 2 tbsp lemon juice

Make the syrup. Put the sugar in a saucepan with 450 ml / 1 pint water. Heat gently, stirring until the sugar has dissolved, then bring to the boil and boil rapidly until the syrup has been reduced by about half. Add the lemon juice, allow to cool, then pour the syrup into a glass serving bowl.

When the syrup is quite cold, add the fruit. Leave the skin on the apples and either slice them or cut them into chunks. Cut the passion fruit in half and scoop out the pulp, straining it to remove the seeds, if preferred. Serve well chilled, decorated with mint.

SERVES FOUR TO SIX

PINEAPPLE AND KIRSCH SALAD

2 small pineapples
100 g / 4 oz black grapes
1 banana
1 pear
15 ml / 1 tbsp lemon juice
30–45 ml / 2–3 tbsp kirsch
sugar

Cut the pineapples in half lengthways. Cut out the core from each, then scoop out the flesh, using first a knife, then a spoon, but taking care to keep the pineapple shells intact. Discard the core, and working over a bowl to catch the juice, chop the flesh.

Add the pineapple flesh to the bowl. Halve the grapes and remove the pips. Add to the pineapple mixture. Peel and slice the banana; peel, core, and slice the pear. Put the lemon juice in a shallow bowl, add the pear and banana slices and toss both fruits before adding to the pineapple and grapes.

Mix all the fruit together, pour the kirsch over and sweeten to taste with the sugar. Pile the fruit back into the pineapple shells and chill until required.

SERVES FOUR

MRS BEETON'S TRIFLE

Plain whisked or creamed sponge cake, individual buns, or Madeira cake are ideal for this trifle. Originally, Mrs Beeton made her custard by using 8 eggs to thicken 600 ml / 1 pint milk, cooking it slowly over hot water. Using cornflour and egg yolks is more practical and it gives a creamier, less 'eggy' result.

4 slices of plain cake or individual cakes
6 almond macaroons
12 ratafias
175 ml / 6 fl oz sherry
30–45 ml / 2–3 tbsp brandy
60–90 ml / 4–6 tbsp raspberry or strawberry jam
grated rind of 1 lemon
25 g / 1 oz flaked almonds
300 ml / ½ pint double cream
30 ml / 2 tbsp icing sugar
candied and crystallized fruit and peel to decorate

CUSTARD
25 g / 1 oz cornflour
25 g / 1 oz caster sugar
4 egg yolks
5 ml / 1 tsp vanilla essence
600 ml / 1 pint milk

Place the sponge cakes in a glass dish. Add the macaroons and ratafias, pressing them down gently. Pour about 50 ml / 2 fl oz of the sherry into a basin and set it aside, then pour the rest over the biscuits and cake. Sprinkle with the brandy. Warm the jam in a small saucepan, then pour it evenly over the trifle base, spreading it lightly. Top with the lemon rind and almonds.

For the custard, blend the cornflour, caster sugar, egg yolks and vanilla to a smooth cream with a little of the milk. Heat the remaining milk until hot. Pour some of the milk on the egg mixture, stirring, then replace the mixture in the saucepan with the rest of the milk. Bring to the boil, stirring constantly, and simmer for 3 minutes.

Pour the custard over the trifle base and cover the surface with a piece of dampened greaseproof paper. Set aside to cool.

Add the cream and icing sugar to the reserved sherry and whip until the mixture stands in soft peaks. Swirl the cream over the top of the trifle and chill. Decorate with pieces of candied and crystallized fruit and peel before serving.

SERVES SIX

BANANAS IN RUM

45 ml / 3 tbsp soft light brown sugar
2.5 ml / ¼ tsp ground cinnamon
4 large bananas
25 g / 1 oz butter
45–60 ml / 3–4 tbsp rum
150 ml / ¼ pint double cream to serve

Mix the sugar and cinnamon in a shallow dish. Cut the bananas in half lengthways and dredge them in the sugar and cinnamon mixture.

Melt the butter in a frying pan and fry the bananas, flat side down, for 1–2 minutes or until lightly browned underneath. Turn them over carefully, sprinkle with any remaining sugar and cinnamon and continue frying.

When the bananas are soft but not mushy, pour the rum over them. Tilt the pan and baste the bananas, then ignite the rum; baste again. Scrape any caramelized sugar from the base of the pan and stir it into the rum sauce. Shake the pan gently until the flames die down.

Arrange the bananas on warmed plates, pour the rum sauce over the top and serve with cream.

SERVES FOUR

PEARS IN WINE

100 g / 4 oz sugar
30 ml / 2 tbsp redcurrant jelly
1.5 cm / ¾ inch cinnamon stick
4 large ripe cooking pears (about 450 g / 1 lb)
250 ml / 8 fl oz red wine
25 g / 1 oz flaked almonds

Combine the sugar, redcurrant jelly and cinnamon stick in a saucepan wide enough to hold all the pears upright so that they fit snugly and will not fall over. Add 250 ml / 8 fl oz water and heat gently, stirring, until the sugar and jelly have dissolved.

Peel the pears, leaving the stalks in place. Carefully remove as much of the core as possible without breaking the fruit. Stand the pears upright in the pan, cover, and simmer gently for 15 minutes.

Add the wine and cook, uncovered, for 15 minutes more. Remove the pears carefully with a slotted spoon, arrange them on a serving dish.

Remove the cinnamon stick from the pan and add the almonds. Boil the liquid remaining in the pan rapidly until it is reduced to a thin syrup. Pour the syrup over the pears and serve warm. This dessert can also be served cold. Pour the hot syrup over the pears, leave to cool, then chill before serving.

SERVES FOUR

CHERRIES JUBILEE

This famous dish was created for Queen Victoria's Diamond Jubilee. It is often finished at the table, with the cherries and sauce kept warm in a chafing dish and the kirsch ignited and added at the last moment.

50 g / 2 oz sugar
450 g / 1 lb dark red cherries, stoned
10 ml / 2 tsp arrowroot
60 ml / 4 tbsp kirsch

Put the sugar in a heavy-bottomed saucepan. Add 250 ml / 8 fl oz water. Heat gently, stirring, until the sugar has dissolved, then boil steadily without stirring for 3–4 minutes to make a syrup. Lower the heat, add the cherries and poach gently until tender. Using a slotted spoon, remove the cherries from the pan and set them aside on a plate to cool.

In a cup, mix the arrowroot with about 30 ml / 2 tbsp of the syrup to a thin paste. Stir back into the pan. Bring to the boil, stirring constantly, until the mixture thickens. Remove from the heat.

Pile the cherries in a heatproof serving bowl. Pour the sauce over them. Heat the kirsch in a small saucepan or ladle. Ignite it, pour it over the cherries and serve at once.

SERVES FOUR

PINEAPPLE BUTTERMILK WHIP

This is a very good dessert for slimmers.

400 ml / 14 fl oz unsweetened pineapple or orange juice
15 ml / 1 tbsp gelatine
150 ml / ¼ pint buttermilk

Place 60 ml / 4 tbsp of the fruit juice in a small bowl and sprinkle the gelatine on to the liquid. Set aside for 15 minutes until the gelatine is spongy. Stand the bowl over a saucepan of hot water and stir continuously the gelatine until it has dissolved completely.

Combine the gelatine mixture with the remaining fruit juice. Pour a little of the mixture into each of 4 stemmed glasses.

Chill the rest of the juice mixture for about 1 hour. When it is on the point of setting, whisk in the buttermilk until frothy. Spoon into the glasses and chill.

SERVES FOUR

MRS BEETON'S TIP

Take care, when adding the creamy mixture to the glasses, not to disturb the jelly layer.

RHUBARB AND BANANA FOOL

450 g / 1 lb young rhubarb
75 g / 3 oz soft light brown sugar
piece of pared lemon rind
6 bananas
caster sugar (see method)
250 ml / 8 fl oz cold Cornflour Custard Sauce (page 228), or lightly whipped double cream
ratafias, to decorate

Remove any strings from the rhubarb and cut the stalks into 2.5 cm / 1 inch lengths. Put into the top of a double saucepan and stir in the brown sugar and lemon rind. Set the pan over simmering water and cook for 10–15 minutes until the rhubarb is soft. Remove the lemon rind.

Meanwhile peel the bananas and purée in a blender or food processor. Add the rhubarb and process briefly until mixed. Alternatively, mash the bananas in a bowl and stir in the cooked rhubarb. Taste the mixture and add caster sugar, if necessary.

Fold the custard or cream into the fruit purée and turn into a serving bowl. Decorate with ratafias.

SERVES SIX TO EIGHT

MRS BEETON'S TIP

If time permits, cook the rhubarb very slowly overnight. Layer the fruit in a casserole, add the sugar and lemon rind. Do not add any liquid. Cover and bake at 110°C / 225°F / gas ¼.

TORTA DI RICOTTA

BASE

100 g / 4 oz butter or margarine
75 g / 3 oz icing sugar
2 egg yolks
pinch of ground cinnamon
250 g / 9 oz plain flour
flour for rolling out

FILLING

675 g / 1½ lb ricotta cheese
25 g / 1 oz grated Parmesan cheese
2 eggs
25 g / 1 oz plain flour
45 ml / 3 tbsp plain yogurt
50 g / 2 oz caster sugar
grated rind and juice of 1 lemon
pinch of salt
few drops of lemon essence

DECORATION AND SAUCE

225 g / 8 oz fresh raspberries
15 ml / 1 tbsp arrowroot
100 g / 4 oz raspberry jam
60 ml / 4 tbsp maraschino liqueur
125 ml / 4 fl oz sweet red vermouth

Make the pastry. Cream the butter or margarine with the sugar in a mixing bowl until light and fluffy. Blend in the egg yolks, cinnamon and flour. Knead the mixture lightly and roll into a ball. Chill for 20 minutes.

Set the oven at 200°C / 400°F / gas 6. Roll out the pastry on a lightly floured surface to line a 25-cm / 10-inch flan ring set on a baking sheet (see Mrs Beeton's Tip). Prick the base with a fork and chill for 30 minutes. Line with greaseproof paper and sprinkle with baking beans or dried peas. Bake for 20 minutes; remove paper and beans or peas. Lower the oven temperature to 180°C / 350°F / gas 4.

For the filling, rub the ricotta through a sieve, then beat it with the Parmesan in a bowl and gradually beat in the rest of the filling ingredients. Spoon into the partially cooked flan case, level the surface and bake for about 50 minutes. Cover loosely with foil if the top becomes too dark. The filling should be firmly set when cooked. Leave to cool in the tin.

Decorate the cooled flan with the raspberries, and chill while making the sauce. Put the arrowroot in a small bowl and mix to a thin cream with 125 ml / 4 fl oz water. Melt the jam in a saucepan. When it boils, stir in the arrowroot mixture to thicken it. Flavour with the maraschino liqueur and vermouth. Remove from the heat and when cold, pour a little of the sauce over the raspberries. Serve the rest separately.

SERVES EIGHT

MRS BEETON'S TIP

To line the flan ring, place on the baking sheet and roll the pastry to a round at least 5 cm / 2 inches larger than the ring. The pastry should be about 3 mm / ⅛ inch thick. Lift the pastry round over a rolling pin to prevent it breaking and stretching, and lay it in the flan ring. Press the pastry gently down on the baking sheet and into the base of the ring. Working from the centre outwards, press the pastry into the base and up the sides, making sure it fits snugly into the flutes, if present, and is of even thickness all round. Trim off any surplus pastry by rolling across the top of the ring with the rolling pin.

COEUR À LA CRÈME AU CITRON

150 ml / ¼ pint double cream
pinch of salt
150 g / 5 oz low-fat curd cheese
50 g / 2 oz caster sugar
grated rind and juice of 1 lemon
2 egg whites

Line a 400-ml / 14-fl oz heart-shaped coeur à la crème mould with greaseproof paper. In a bowl whip the cream with the salt until it holds soft peaks. Break up the curd cheese with a fork, and whisk it gradually into the cream with the sugar. Do not let the mixture lose stiffness. Fold the lemon rind and juice into the cream as lightly as possible.

In a clean, grease-free bowl, whisk the egg whites until they hold stiff peaks. Fold them into the mixture, then very gently turn the mixture into the mould, filling all the corners.

Stand the mould in a large dish or roasting tin to catch the liquid which seeps from the mixture. Chill for at least 2 hours or overnight. Turn out and serve with single cream.

SERVES SIX

MRS BEETON'S TIP

Individual coeur à la crème moulds may be used. If these are unavailable, clean yogurt pots, with several drainage holes punched in the base of each, make an acceptable substitute.

CLASSIC BAKED CHEESECAKE

BASE

75 g / 3 oz butter
150 g / 5 oz fine white breadcrumbs, dried
50 g / 2 oz caster sugar
7.5 ml / 1½ tsp ground cinnamon

FILLING

3 eggs, separated
100 g / 4 oz caster sugar
375 g / 13 oz full-fat soft cheese
grated rind and juice of 1 lemon
125 ml / 4 fl oz soured cream
icing sugar for dusting

Set the oven at 180°C / 350°F / gas 4. Make the base. Melt the butter in a frying pan and stir in the breadcrumbs. Cook over gentle heat, stirring until the crumbs are golden. Remove from the heat; stir in the sugar and cinnamon. Press the crumbs over the base of a loose-bottomed 18-cm / 7-inch cake tin.

Beat the egg yolks in a mixing bowl until liquid. Add the sugar to the egg yolks, beating until creamy. Rub the cheese through a sieve into the bowl, then work in lightly. Add the lemon rind and juice to the mixture with the soured cream.

In a clean, grease-free bowl, whisk the egg whites to soft peaks. Stir 30 ml / 2 tbsp into the cheese mixture, then fold in the rest lightly. Turn the mixture gently on to the prepared base in the tin. Bake for 45 minutes. Cover loosely with foil and bake for a further 15 minutes. Cool in the tin. Serve dusted with icing sugar.

SERVES TEN

VELVET CREAM

This basic recipe produces one of the simplest and most delicious of desserts, the full cream. It lends itself to a wide range of variations and may be served in glasses or as a decorative mould (see Mrs Beeton's Tip).

10 ml / 2 tsp gelatine
50 g / 2 oz caster sugar
30 ml / 2 tbsp sherry or a few drops of vanilla essence
250 ml / 8 fl oz double cream
250 ml / 8 fl oz single cream

Place 45 ml / 3 tbsp water in a small bowl and sprinkle the gelatine on to the liquid. Set aside for 15 minutes until the gelatine is spongy. Stand the bowl over a saucepan of hot water and stir the gelatine until it has dissolved completely. Add the sugar and sherry or vanilla essence and continue to stir until the sugar has dissolved. Set aside.

Combine the creams in a mixing bowl and whip lightly. Fold the flavoured gelatine mixture into the cream and divide between 4 glasses or individual dishes. Refrigerate for 1–2 hours or until set. When the cream has set, a thin top layer of fresh fruit jelly may be added, if liked.

SERVES FOUR

VARIATIONS

In each of the variations below, omit the sherry or vanilla essence.

- **Almond Cream** Flavour with 1.25 ml / ¼ tsp almond essence. Decorate with browned almonds.
- **Berry Cream** Use 375 ml / 13 fl oz double cream and fold in 125 ml / 4 fl oz raspberry or strawberry purée instead of single cream. Decorate with fresh berry fruits.
- **Chocolate Cream** Flavour with 75 g / 3 oz melted plain chocolate. Decorate the top with chocolate curls.
- **Coffee Cream** Flavour with 15 ml / 1 tbsp instant coffee dissolved in 15 ml / 1 tbsp boiling water and cooled. Add 15 ml / 1 tbsp rum, if liked, and decorate with coffee beans.
- **Highland Cream** Flavour with 15 ml / 1 tbsp whisky and serve with a whisky-spiked apricot sauce.
- **Lemon and Almond Cream** Flavour with 30 ml / 2 tbsp lemon juice, 5 ml / 1 tsp grated lemon rind and 25 g / 1 oz ground almonds.
- **Liqueur Cream** Flavour with 15 ml / 1 tbsp Tia Maria, curaçao, kirsch or Advocaat.
- **Pistachio Cream** Blanch, skin and finely chop 100 g / 4 oz pistachio nuts and fold into the mixture before adding the gelatine. Tint the cream pale green with food colouring.

MRS BEETON'S TIP

The cream may be made in a mould, if preferred. Make up a packet of lemon jelly. Use some of the jelly to line a 750-ml / 1 ¼-pint mould, decorating it with cut shapes of angelica and glacé cherry. When the jelly lining has set, carefully add the prepared cream and refrigerate for 2–3 hours until set. The remaining jelly may be set in a shallow tray, then chopped for use as a decoration.

CRÈME BRÛLÉE À LA GRANDE CATELET

An ideal dinner party dish. If serving cold, tap the caramel crust sharply with the back of a spoon to break it up.

250 ml / 8 fl oz single cream or milk
250 ml / 8 fl oz double cream
1 vanilla pod or a few drops of vanilla essence or 15 ml / 1 tbsp brandy
6 egg yolks
about 75 g / 3 oz caster sugar

Put the cream or milk and the double cream in a double saucepan or a bowl over a saucepan of hot water. Add the vanilla pod, if used, and warm very gently. Meanwhile mix the egg yolks with 25 g / 1 oz of the caster sugar in a large bowl. Beat together thoroughly.

When the cream feels just warm to the finger, remove the pod, if used. Pour the cream on to the yolks, stir, and return to the double saucepan or bowl.

Continue to cook gently for about 40 minutes, stirring all the time with a wooden spoon, until the custard thickens to the consistency of single cream (see Mrs Beeton's Tip). Do not let the custard approach the boiling point. If a vanilla pod has not been used, add a few drops of vanilla essence or the brandy. Set the oven at 160°C / 325°F / gas 3.

Strain the custard into a shallow 600-ml / 1-pint flameproof dish, stand it on a baking sheet and bake for 5–10 minutes until a skin has formed on the top.

MRS BEETON'S TIP

When cooking the custard scrape down the sides of the saucepan frequently with a spatula to prevent the formation of lumps.

Do not allow the custard to colour. Leave to cool, then refrigerate for at least 2–3 hours, or preferably overnight.

Heat the grill. Sprinkle enough of the remaining caster sugar over the surface of the custard to cover it entirely with an even, thin layer. Place the dish under the hot grill for 10–15 minutes or until the sugar melts and turns to caramel. Keep the top of the custard about 10 cm / 4 inches from the heat. Serve hot or cold.

SERVES FOUR

FRENCH CHOCOLATE CREAMS

This is incredibly rich, so a little goes a long way.

150 ml / ¼ pint milk
60 ml / 4 tbsp caster sugar
pinch of salt
100 g / 4 oz plain chocolate, coarsely grated
100 g / 4 oz unsalted butter, in small pieces
8 egg yolks

Warm the milk, sugar and salt in a small saucepan and stir until the sugar dissolves. Set the pan aside.

Combine the chocolate and butter in a large heatproof bowl and place over hot water. Heat gently, stirring constantly, until the mixture is quite smooth and all the solids have melted.

Add the milk to the chocolate mixture, stirring it in thoroughly. Using a balloon whisk if possible, beat in the egg yolks one at a time. On no account allow the mixture to curdle.

Divide the cream between 6 small pots or ramekins. Chill well before serving.

SERVES SIX

CARAMEL CUSTARD CUPS

100 g / 4 oz lump or granulated sugar
300 ml / ½ pint milk
100 ml / 3½ fl oz single cream
2 whole eggs and 2 yolks
25 g / 1 oz caster sugar
few drops of vanilla essence

Prepare four 150-ml / ¼-pint ovenproof moulds to receive a caramel coating (see Mrs Beeton's Tip).

Make the caramel by heating the lump sugar with 150 ml / ¼ pint water in a heavy-bottomed saucepan. Stir constantly until the sugar dissolves and the mixture comes to the boil. Continue to boil, without stirring, until the mixture is golden brown. Pour a little of the caramel on to a metal plate and set aside. Immediately pour the remaining caramel into the warmed moulds, twisting and turning each mould in turn until the sides and the base are evenly coated. Leave until cold and set. Set the oven at 140–150°C / 275–300°F / gas 1–2.

In a saucepan, bring the milk and cream to just below boiling point. Put the eggs and sugar into a bowl, mix well, then stir in the scalded milk. Add a few drops of vanilla essence. Strain the custard mixture into the prepared moulds.

MRS BEETON'S TIP

Hot caramel can cause nasty burns. The best way to safeguard yourself is by using a newspaper holder: prepare a thickly folded band of newspaper long enough to encircle the chosen mould. Heat the mould in boiling water or in the oven, then wrap the newspaper around it, twisting the ends tightly to form a handle. Make sure that the band is secure and the ends are tight enough to prevent slipping. Hold the paper, not the side of the mould, when tilting it to distribute the caramel and, as an additional safeguard, work over the sink.

Stand the moulds in a roasting tin and add hot water to come halfway up the sides of the moulds. Bake for 30 minutes or until the custard is set.

Remove the cooked custards and leave to stand for a few minutes, then invert each on an individual dessert plate. The caramel will run off and serve as a sauce. Break up the reserved caramel by tapping sharply with a metal spoon, and decorate the top of each custard with the pieces of broken caramel.

SERVES FOUR

ZABAGLIONE

4 egg yolks
40 g / 1½ oz caster sugar
60 ml / 4 tbsp Marsala or Madeira

Put the egg yolks into a deep heatproof bowl and whisk lightly. Add the sugar and wine, and place the bowl over a saucepan of hot water. Whisk for about 10 minutes or until the mixture is very thick and creamy (when the whisk is lifted, its trails should remain on top of the mixture for a few seconds).

Pour the custard into individual glasses and serve while still warm, accompanied by sponge fingers.

SERVES FOUR

VARIATION

- **Zabaglione Cream** Dissolve 50 g / 2 oz caster sugar in 60 ml / 4 tbsp water in a saucepan and boil for 1–2 minutes until syrupy. Whisk with the egg yolks until pale and thick. Add 30 ml / 2 tbsp Marsala or Madeira and 30 ml / 2 tbsp single cream while whisking. The finely grated rind of ½ lemon can be added, if liked. Spoon into individual glasses and chill before serving.

CRÊPES SUZETTE

100 g / 4 oz unsalted butter
75 g / 3 oz caster sugar
grated rind and juice of 1 lemon
5 ml / 1 tsp lemon juice
15 ml / 1 tbsp orange liqueur
45 ml / 3 tbsp brandy for flaming

CRÊPES
100 g / 4 oz plain flour
1.25 ml / ¼ tsp salt
1 egg, beaten
250 ml / 8 fl oz milk, or half milk and half water
15 g / ½ oz butter, melted and cooled
oil for frying

Make the crêpe batter. Sift the flour and salt into a bowl, make a well in the centre and add the beaten egg. Stir in half the milk (or all the milk, if using a mixture of milk and water), gradually working the flour down from the sides of the bowl.

Beat vigorously until the mixture is smooth and bubbly, then stir in the rest of the milk (or the water). Pour into a jug. The mixture may be left to stand at this stage, in which case it should be covered and stored in the refrigerator.

Heat a little oil in a clean 18-cm / 7-inch pancake pan. Pour off any excess oil, leaving the pan covered with a thin film of grease.

Stir the melted butter into the batter and pour about 30–45 ml / 2–3 tbsp into the pan. There should be just enough to cover the base thinly. Tilt and rotate the pan so that the batter runs over the surface evenly.

Cook over moderate heat for about 1 minute until the crêpe is set and golden brown underneath. Make sure the crêpe is loose by shaking the pan, then either toss it or turn it with a palette knife or fish slice. Cook the second side for about 30 seconds or until golden.

Slide the crêpe out on to a plate and keep warm over simmering water while making 7 more crêpes in the same way. Add more oil to the pan when necessary.

Make the filling by creaming the unsalted butter with the sugar in a bowl. Beat in the orange rind, lemon juice and liqueur, with enough of the orange juice to give a soft, creamy consistency.

Spread the filling over the cooked crêpes, dividing it evenly between them. Fold each crêpe in half, then in half again to make a quarter circle.

Return half the crêpes to the pan and warm through for 1–2 minutes. As the orange butter melts and runs out, spoon it over the crêpes. Pour in half the brandy, tip the pan to one side and increase the heat. Ignite the brandy and serve at once, with the pan sauce. Repeat with the remaining crêpes and brandy.

SERVES FOUR

LEMON DELICIOUS PUDDING

This pudding has a light spongy top with lemon sauce underneath.

butter for greasing
3 eggs, separated
75 g / 3 oz caster sugar
200 ml / 7 fl oz milk
15 ml / 1 tbsp self-raising flour, sifted
grated rind and juice of 2 large lemons
pinch of salt
15 ml / 1 tbsp icing sugar

Grease a deep 1-litre / 1¾-pint ovenproof dish. Set the oven at 180°C / 350°F / gas 4.

In a mixing bowl, beat the egg yolks together with the caster sugar until light, pale and creamy. Whisk the milk, flour, rind and lemon juice into the egg yolks. In a clean, grease-free bowl, whisk the egg whites with the salt, adding the icing sugar gradually. Continue to whisk until stiff but not dry. Fold into the lemon mixture.

Pour the mixture into the prepared dish and stand the dish in a roasting tin. Add hot water to come halfway up the sides of the dish. Bake for 1 hour.

SERVES FOUR

MRS BEETON'S TIP

If a fragment of shell drops into the egg white, the easiest way to remove it is to use another piece of shell.

EVE'S PUDDING

butter for greasing
450 g / 1 lb cooking apples
grated rind and juice of 1 lemon
75 g / 3 oz demerara sugar
75 g / 3 oz butter or margarine
75 g / 3 oz caster sugar
1 egg. beaten
100 g / 4 oz self-raising flour

Grease a 1-litre / 1¾-pint pie dish. Set the oven at 180°C / 350°F / gas 4. Peel and core the apples and slice them thinly into a large bowl. Add the lemon rind and juice, with the demerara sugar. Stir in 15 ml / 1 tbsp water, then tip the mixture into the prepared pie dish.

In a mixing bowl, cream the butter or margarine with the caster sugar until light and fluffy. Beat in the egg. Fold in the flour lightly and spread the mixture over the apples.

Bake for 40–45 minutes until the apples are soft and the sponge is firm. Serve with melted apple jelly and single cream or Greek yogurt.

SERVES FOUR

VARIATIONS

- Instead of apples, use 450 g / 1 lb, apricots, peaches, gooseberries, rhubarb, raspberries or plums.

APPLE CRUMBLE

butter for greasing
675 g / 1½ lb cooking apples
100 g / 4 oz granulated sugar
grated rind of 1 lemon
150 g / 5 oz plain flour
75 g / 3 oz butter or margarine
75 g / 3 oz caster sugar
1.25 ml / ¼ tsp ground ginger

Grease a 1-litre / 1¾-pint pie dish. Set the oven at 180°C / 350°F / gas 4. Peel and core the apples. Slice into a saucepan and add the granulated sugar and lemon rind. Stir in 50 ml / 2 fl oz water, cover the pan and cook until the apples are soft. Spoon the apple mixture into the prepared dish and set aside.

Put the flour into a mixing bowl and rub in the butter or margarine until the mixture resembles fine breadcrumbs. Add the caster sugar and ginger and stir well. Sprinkle the mixture over the apples and press down lightly. Bake for 30–40 minutes until the crumble topping is golden brown.

SERVES SIX

VARIATIONS

- Instead of apples, use 675 g / 1½ lb damsons, gooseberries, pears, plums, rhubarb or raspberries.

MICROWAVE TIP

Put the apple mixture in a large bowl, adding only 30 ml / 2 tbsp water, cover and cook for 7 minutes on High. Add the crumble topping and cook for 4 minutes more, then brown the topping under a preheated grill.

GANACHE TRUFFLES

Ganache is a rich chocolate cream, made by melting chocolate with cream, then allowing it to set. The chocolate cream may be whipped before it is firm to make a rich topping for cakes; for truffles the mixture is chilled until it is firm enough to be shaped and coated.

350 g / 12 oz plain chocolate
300 ml / ½ pint double cream
5 ml / 1 tsp vanilla essence
15 ml / 1 tbsp icing sugar
cocoa for coating

Break the chocolate into squares and place them in a small saucepan. Add the cream and heat gently, stirring often, until the chocolate melts. Remove from the heat and stir in the vanilla, then allow to cool, stirring occasionally.

Chill the mixture until it is firm enough to shape. Place the cocoa in a small basin. Use two teaspoons to shape small balls of mixture and drop them in the cocoa one at a time. Turn the truffles in the cocoa to coat them completely, then place them on a plate or baking sheet and chill again until firm.

MAKES ABOUT 25

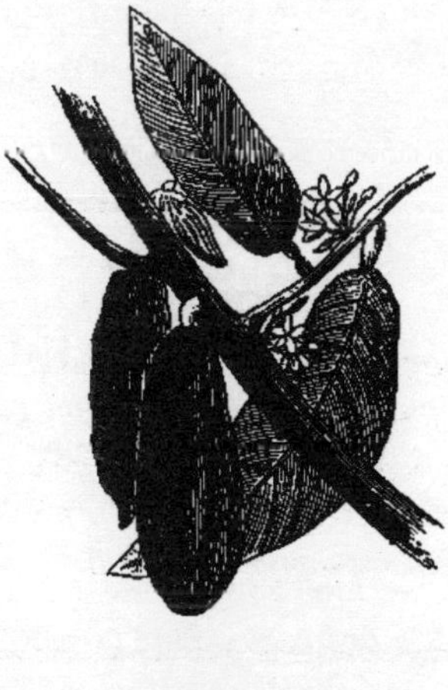

VANILLA CUSTARD

Adding cornflour stabilizes the custard and makes it less inclined to curdle.

10 ml / 2 tsp cornflour
500 ml / 17 fl oz milk
25 g / 1 oz caster sugar
2 eggs
vanilla essence

In a bowl, mix the cornflour to a smooth paste with a little of the cold milk. Heat the rest of the milk in a saucepan and when hot pour it on to the blended cornflour, stirring.

Return to the mixture to the pan, bring to the boil and boil for 1–2 minutes, stirring all the time, to cook the cornflour. Remove from the heat and stir in the sugar. Leave to cool.

Beat the eggs together lightly in a small bowl. Add a little of the cooked cornflour mixture, stir well, then pour into the pan. Heat gently for a few minutes until the custard has thickened, stirring all the time. Do not boil. Stir in a few drops of vanilla essence. Serve hot or cold as an accompaniment to a pudding or pie.

MAKES ABOUT 600 ml / 1 pint

CORNFLOUR CUSTARD SAUCE

15 ml / 1 tbsp cornflour
250ml / 8 fl oz milk
1 egg yolk
15 ml / 1 tbsp sugar
few drops of vanilla essence

Mix the cornflour with a little of the cold milk in a large bowl. Bring the rest of the milk to the boil in a saucepan, then stir into the blended mixture. Return the mixture to the clean pan.

Bring the cornflour mixture to the boil and boil for 3 minutes to cook the cornflour. Remove from the heat.

When the mixture has cooled a little, stir in the egg yolk and sugar. Return to low heat and cook, stirring carefully, until the sauce thickens. Do not let it boil. Flavour with a few drops of vanilla essence and pour into a jug.

MAKES ABOUT 250 ml / 8 fl oz

SIMPLE CUSTARD SAUCE

The addition of cornflour makes it unnecessary to use a double saucepan to make this sauce, provided care is taken to avoid excessive heat and the custard is constantly stirred.

500 ml / 17 fl oz milk
few drops of vanilla essence
6 egg yolks
100 g / 4 oz caster sugar
10 ml / 2 tsp cornflour

Combine the milk and vanilla essence in a saucepan. Warm gently but do not allow to boil.

In a bowl, beat the egg yolks, sugar and cornflour together until creamy. Add the warm milk.

Strain the mixture back into the clean pan and cook, stirring constantly, until the custard thickens and coats the back of the spoon. Serve hot or cold.

MAKES ABOUT 600 ml / 1 pint

CLASSIC EGG CUSTARD SAUCE

This recipe may be used as the basis for ice cream.

500 ml / 17 fl oz milk
few drops of vanilla essence or other flavouring
6 egg yolks
100 g / 4 oz caster sugar

Put the milk in a saucepan with the vanilla or other flavouring. Warm gently but do not let the liquid boil. If a solid flavouring such as a strip of citrus rind is used, allow it to infuse in the milk for 5 minutes, then remove.

In a bowl, beat the egg yolks and sugar together until creamy. Add the warm milk to the egg mixture.

Strain the mixture into a double saucepan or a heatproof bowl placed over a saucepan of simmering water. Cook, stirring constantly with a wooden spoon for 20–30 minutes, until the custard thickens and coats the back of the spoon. Take care not to let the custard curdle. Serve hot or cold.

MAKES ABOUT 500 ml / 17 fl oz

VARIATIONS

- **Classic Lemon Custard** Infuse a thin strip of lemon rind in the milk, removing it before adding to the eggs
- **Classic Orange Custard** Substitute orange for lemon rind
- **Classic Liqueur Custard** Add 15 ml / 1 tbsp kirsch or curaçao at the end of the cooking time.
- **Praline Custard** Stir in crushed praline just before serving. To make praline, heat 100 g / 4 oz sugar with 15 ml / 1 tbsp water until dissolved, then boil until golden. Stir in 100 g / 4 oz toasted blanched almonds and turn the mixture on to an oiled baking sheet to cool. Crush in a mortar with a pestle, or use a blender.

PLANNING A CHEESE COURSE

'A celebrated gourmand remarked that a dinner without cheese is like a woman with one eye.' Isabella Beeton

A cheese course typically features three or four cheeses, served on an open board or platter that can be passed around your guests. Selecting the cheeses is a great opportunity for tasting sessions at your delicatessen counter. A variety of strengths and textures works well; for example, a soft cheese (such as a goat's cheese), a semi-soft cheese (such as Port Salut or Camembert), a hard cheese (such as Applewood Smoked Cheddar), a crumbly white cheese (such as Lancashire or Wensleydale) or a blue cheese (such as strong-tasting Stilton or mild Dolcelatte).

- Serve cheese unwrapped and at room temperature. Arrange the cheese for serving, ensuring there is enough space around each cheese to cut it, and loosely cover by a clean tea towel.
- If you're planning for a large number of guests, provide more than one platter of the same cheeses.
- Provide each guest with a salad or bread plate to put the cheese on as it comes around.
- Special cheese knives are available, but the important thing is to provide knives that will allow for each cheese with a different texture – a sharp knife for semi-hard or hard cheeses and a butter knife for soft cheese. Slices ideally follow the natural lines of the cheese, or are taken like slices of cake from a round cheese.

- Serve crackers, water biscuits, oat cakes and/or interesting breads (those with nuts or fruit make excellent accompaniments). Also provide spreadable butter and margarine.
- If your meal has been relatively light, you might consider extra accompaniments to your cheese course such as grapes, sharp apples, figs, olives, cornichons, chutneys, flavoured oils, mustards, toasted seeds and nuts such as walnuts. It is a good idea to contrast flavours and textures. Try tart apple slices with mild creamy or plain salty cheeses; fresh figs with blue cheese. The region a cheese is from often suggests perfect partners: for example, Spanish Manchego is often teamed with a traditional quince jelly or almonds and sherry, and British Stilton is fantastic with port.
- A reputable cheese merchant is invaluable in giving advice on selection, combination and storage of cheeses, providing tasting samples, taking on board your own feedback and refining your serving ideas.

Table Laying & Menu Planning

TABLE LAYING

Following dining trends, there are many options for table laying, from formal settings to casual, yet attractive presentations.

PLACE SETTINGS

If soup is to be served, round soup spoons or dessert spoons should be provided. Special fish knives and forks can be laid for the fish course; the knives are blunt with a slightly pointed end which enables the bones to be eased out of the fish without cutting the flesh. Large knives and forks are laid for the main meat course, with a small knife for bread and butter and cheese. Steak knives with a serrated cutting edge are often used for grilled steak or chops. A dessertspoon and fork are provided for the sweet course, or a teaspoon if the dessert is to be served in small dishes or glasses. If fresh fruit is being served, the appropriate knives and forks should be provided.

TABLE DECORATIONS

Flower arrangements should be low and flowers must not be overpoweringly scented. Candles should match table linen and/or room decor. Wine should be placed ready on the sideboard or side table together with a jug of iced water and soft drinks. Sauceboats should have a stand or saucer to avoid drips on the tablecloth.

THE BUFFET TABLE

The art of laying a buffet table is to show off the food to its best advantage while making serving easy.

For buffets to serve 50 people or more, place plates and cutlery at either end of the buffet table so that there at least two serving points. This means that there must be two platters (at least) of each dish so that guests may help themselves from either end of the table. Drinks, and later coffee, should be served from a side table. Depending on the space available, the dessert can be displayed ready on a side table, or served from the main table when the main course is finished. Use cake stands for gateau-type desserts to vary the height of the display. The most convenient way to lay cutlery is to wrap a set for each person in a table napkin. Distribute cruets along the table, and accompaniments (salad dressing or sauce) near the appropriate dishes. Place bread or rolls with butter at each end of the table. Cheeseboards should be brought in with the dessert and placed at each end of the buffet with celery, biscuits and butter, and, of course, small plates and knives. For small buffets, it is usually possible to lay everything on one table with cutlery and plates at one end only.

TRADITIONAL FORMAL SETTINGS

Lay the knives, blades pointing inwards, on the right of the dinner plate and the forks on the left in the order in which they will be used (first to be used on the extreme right or left and the last next to the plate). The dessertspoon and fork can either be laid in neat alignment across the top of the setting, with the spoon handle to the right and the fork handle to the left, or at the sides of the plate, spoon on the right, fork on the left; either arrangement is correct. Fruit knives and forks can be laid across the top of the setting with the dessertspoon and fork, or at the side. Alternatively, they can be handed round with the dessert plates. The small knife for bread may go next to the dinner plate, on the right-hand side or vertically across the side plate, which should be on the left of the place setting. The soup spoon is placed on the extreme right-hand side as this is the first implement to be used. Line up the cutlery neatly and as closely together as is practical, with the handles about 1 cm / ½ inch from the edge of the table.

Glasses should be arranged in a straight line across the top of the right-hand cutlery, in the order of use; for example, a glass for white wine on the right, then one for red, and a port or liqueur glass on the left of the row. If you include a tumbler or stemmed glass for water, place this before the liqueur glass. The last glass should be placed just above the meat knife. If you are laying a single wine glass, put it anywhere above the right-hand cutlery.

Finger-bowls, if used, are placed to the left just above the line of forks. Table napkins can be put in the centre of the place setting, on the side plate or in one of the glasses.

ALTERNATIVE SETTINGS

A completely different approach to table laying is sometimes suitable for casual or everyday entertaining. Place mats are widely used instead of tablecloths, on both formal and casual occasions. The table setting may be changed completely to reflect the food as when Chinese bowls, chopsticks, spoons and forks replace the traditional cutlery. For an informal, one-course meal, the cutlery (usually a knife and fork) may be placed neatly together on a napkin on the side plate in the centre of the setting. Match bright china with colourful napkins, flowers or ribbons to emphasize the light-hearted approach.

CUTLERY AND CONDIMENTS

Whatever the type of meal, always make sure the necessary serving utensils are on the table.

Traditionally, serving spoons and forks are paired at both ends of the table, according to the number of dishes, arranged as for the dessert cutlery. Have all the implements for serving the main course on the table; those for the dessert may be brought in later.

Salt and pepper, or just a pepper mill, and any other condiments or accompaniments, should be positioned centrally but to one side of the table. For a large dinner party, it is customary to have more than one set of condiments and two plates of butter. Place a butter knife near the butter.

MENU PLANNING

The success of any snack or meal, both in aesthetic and dietary terms, hinges upon the combination of food or dishes which comprise it. A few important guideline summarize the approach to planning menus for every day as well as for special occasions.

The key points to consider when planning a menu, apart from the likes and dislikes or dietary restrictions of the diners, are the flavours, textures, colour and weight of the meal. A well-planned menu balances all these elements. Additional practical aspects to consider are your ability and confidence as a cook; the budget for one meal or for a weekly – or monthly – run of meals; and the cooking facilities available.

When planning a menu, it is usual to consider the main course of the meal first, then to fit the starter, fish course or dessert around it. This does not always have to be the rule – if you have a particularly splendid starter or dessert which you want to serve at a dinner party, or even for a family meal, there is absolutely no reason why you should not work the rest of the meal around it. If, for example, you wanted to serve a chocolate fondue as the finale of a dinner party, it would be logical to keep the preceding courses light. Equally, a traditional steamed sponge pudding with custard is a real family treat but is not suitable for serving after a very filling main course, so a light salad and grilled fish would be the better option.

FLAVOURS AND TEXTURES

As well as considering the accompaniments for the main dish, remember that a strongly flavoured starter will put a lightly seasoned main course in the shade, just as a very spicy main course will ruin the palate for a delicate dessert. Balance strong flavours and aim to accentuate more subtle dishes.

Texture is a less obvious but equally important characteristic of food. A meal that consists solely of soft food is dull, and three courses of dry or crunchy dishes can be a disaster, leaving everyone gasping for water. Balance soft and smooth mixtures with crunchy textures; combine moist dishes with dry ones. Offer crisp salads with zesty dressings to counteract rich fried foods; serve plain, crunchy, lightly cooked vegetables to balance heavily-sauced casseroles and stews.

COLOUR AND WEIGHT

The importance of colour in a dish and on a menu does not simply refer to the piece of parsley dropped on to a grey sauce. The ingredients used in individual dishes, the quality of cooking juices and sauces and the choice of accompaniments are all factors in achieving a menu that looks appealing. Some cooked foods inevitably look uninteresting; this is when the choice of accompaniments is vital. Remember that flavour and texture must also be considered.

The overall weight of the meal is important. Light dishes should balance richer foods. A filling dish should always be flanked by delicate courses.

FOOD VALUE

Dinner parties and special meals are occasions for breaking or bending the rules and indulging in favourite foods. When planning everyday meals or snacks, however, it is very important to consider food value alongside the flavour, texture and appearance of the dishes. Applying rigid guidelines to every meal is not practical, but considering the overall food value of the day's diet is prudent. Taking a sensible overall view of food eaten over a period of a few days, or within a week, is also a reasonable way of ensuring that snacks and meals provide a balanced diet. From breakfast through to supper, whether considering the main meal of the day or an in-between meal snack, variety is one of the keys to success, both in the range of foods eaten and the cooking or serving methods used.

CATERING FOR SPECIAL DIETS

Be aware of any dietary restrictions for social or medical reasons, planning them into the menu for all diners as far as possible. In some cases, for example when catering for vegetarians as well as meat eaters, it is quite possible to provide one menu to suit everyone. Contemporary vegetarian dishes are acceptable to all, not simply to those who avoid animal products; it is far trickier to plan a vegan menu to suit all tastes. Limitations imposed for health reasons may be more difficult to accommodate; if in doubt, check details with the prospective guest or consult an official source of information for guidance.

If the whole menu cannot be adapted to suit everyone, plan the meal around one or two of the key dishes. It is usually quite easy to serve a first course to suit all diets. Either the main dish or vegetable accompaniments should be selected for their versatility: if the main dish is unsuitable for certain diners, then the vegetable accompaniments should make equally interesting main dishes on their own. For example, ratatouille, a mixed vegetable gratin or stir-fried vegetables with noodles are all suitable for serving with plain meat dishes but they are equally good vegetarian dishes when served with appropriate accompaniments.

Adopt this approach whenever you plan meals and snacks, but pay special attention to the food value of restricted diets if you cater for them on a regular basis. Make up for nutrients lost in banned foods by including compensatory alternatives.

PARTIES

The choice of party food depends on the number of guests and the budget – these factors influence the style of food, choice of ingredients, balance of hot and cold dishes and the number of courses. Whether you are planning a formal meal or cocktail-style buffet with snacks and nibbles, remember the following points as they are crucial to the success – or failure – of the menu.

- Time available for food preparation.
- Refrigerator space for storing ingredients and/or dishes requiring chilling.
- Kitchen facilities, particularly oven and hob space.
- Freezer space and suitability of dishes for preparing in advance.
- Availability of crockery and cutlery for serving.
- The time available for last-minute work, finishing dishes, garnishing, etc.
- Your own ability as cook – opt for a menu which you will tackle with confidence.

- Ease of serving and eating the food: the only thing worse than a host or hostess who is overstretched by last-minute cooking between courses at a formal dinner party is the poor guest who is struggling with a knife and fork while standing and balancing a plate, glass and napkin, at the same time chatting politely to other guests.

ADAPTING RECIPES

There are a number of important factors to bear in mind when catering in quantity. If you are planning to scale up a favourite recipe, first look at it carefully to see if it contains any strong flavourings. These do not need to be scaled up in the same proportions as the meat or vegetable content of the recipe, as a small amount of flavouring will penetrate quite large quantities of food. Spices, garlic, strong herbs, and proprietary sauces all need to be handled with care.

The liquid content of the dish also needs to be looked at carefully. A fish dish with sauce, for example, will not need as much sauce when produced in quantity. Stews and casseroles, too, may not need the same proportion of liquid.

Apart from the logical reasons for these differences when increasing quantities, there is also a psychological factor. When dishes are prepared for four or six people, the cook wishes the food not only to be sufficient but to look sufficient, and very often enough food is made for five or seven. Unless this factor is taken into account when scaling up, the resultant recipe for fifty would actually feed sixty or more.

APPROXIMATE QUANTITIES OF BASIC FOODS PER PERSON

Bread	*French bread:* 2 slices (with dinner; more may be eaten with salad); 3–4 slices (served with just wine and cheese) *Rolls:* 2
Butter	25 g / 1 oz
Soup	150 ml / ¼ pint
Meat	*On the bone:* 150–225 g / 5–8 oz (main course: depending on whether used in casserole with vegetables or on its own) *Off the bone:* 100–150 g / 4–5 oz (main course: depending on whether used in casserole with vegetables or on its own)

Chicken	*On the bone:* 150–225 g / 5–8 oz (main course: depending on whether used in casserole with vegetables or on its own) *Off the bone:* 100–150 g / 4–5 oz (main course: depending on whether used in casserole with vegetables or on its own)
Cheese	100 g / 4 oz (served at wine and cheese party); 50 g / 2 oz (served as last course of dinner)
Pâté	50 g / 2 oz (as first-course dish)
Fish	Fillet or steak 100–150 g / 4–5 oz (depending on whether main or subsidiary course)
Vegetables	100 g / 4 oz (served with one other vegetable and potatoes as accompaniment to main course)
Rice	25–50 g / 1–2 oz (uncooked)
Pasta	50–100 g / 2–4 oz (depending on whether main or subsidiary course)
Gravy/sauces	75–100 ml / 3–3½ fl oz (served with main dish)
Salad dressings	15–20 ml / 3–4 tsp (smaller quantity for French dressing, larger for mayonnaise)
Ice cream	50–75 ml / 2–3 fl oz (depending on richness, whether an accompaniment, etc)
Fruit	150 g / 5 oz (for fruit salad)
Pouring cream	75 ml / 3 fl oz
Tea	5 ml / 1 tsp tea leaves; 125 ml / 4 fl oz milk serves 4
Coffee	125 ml / 4 fl oz per person; 125 ml / 4 fl oz cream serves 4

For finger buffets and cocktail canapes, check by making a mental picture of one of each of all the items you are planning to serve set out together on a plate. This will give you an idea of the quantity allowed for each person.

OUTDOOR EATING

The days of the Great British Picnic, when teams of servants set up groaning tables in field and forest, may have passed, but eating out of doors can still be a significant social occasion, with several families or friends gathering for an outdoor party or a sophisticated meal at a sporting event or an alfresco theatrical performance.

Food which can be cooked ahead and eaten cold, salads that travel well without becoming limp and crusty bread are all ideal. Make sure the food arrives in prime condition by using chiller bags for perishable foods. Sturdy plastic containers which seal well are ideal for salads and desserts as well as savouries such as stuffed vine leaves or an array of cooked cold meats.

When ease of preparation takes priority over economy, shop for salami, cooked ham, pork pie, cooked continental sausages, smoked chicken or turkey and smoked mackerel, trout or salmon. Opt for thinly sliced rye breads and a variety of rolls, then make a good mixed salad and take a jar of dressing to toss into it at the last minute.

Finger foods, selected for their portability, are always acceptable. Tiny pizzas, individual filo pastries, quiches or pasties, spiced chicken drumsticks, crudites with a selection of dips, pinwheel sandwiches, filled bridge rolls or prawns will all prove popular.

BARBECUES

Make sure that you have sufficient charcoal and enough grilling space for the food to be cooked. Light the barbecue at least 30 minutes before you plan to cook: depending on the size barbecue, you may need to light it up to 1 hour ahead. The barbecue is ready for cooking when the coals have stopped flaming. When cooking for a crowd of people, part cook chicken in the oven and finish it on the barbecue.

Plan your menu around the barbecuing: have nibbles and drinks for guests while the food is cooking. Dips and crudités are ideal starters. Serve salads, baked potatoes or crusty bread as accompaniments. Have relishes and chutneys with plain grilled foods. Desserts should be simple and fruit may be grilled on the barbecue.

Pay special attention to safety at all times, from lighting up to over-imbibing and risking an accident. Always ensure children are supervised and pets restrained.

Useful Weights and Measures

USING METRIC OR IMPERIAL MEASURES

Throughout the book, all weights and measures are given first in metric, then in imperial. For example 100 g / 4 oz, 150 ml/ ¼ pint or 15 ml / 1 tbsp.

When following any of the recipes use either metric or imperial – do not combine the two sets of measures as they are approximate equivalents, not interchangeable.

EQUIVALENT METRIC / IMPERIAL MEASURES

Weights The following chart lists some of the metric / imperial weights that are used in the recipes.

METRIC	IMPERIAL	METRIC	IMPERIAL
15 g	½ oz	375 g	13 oz
25 g	1 oz	400 g	14 oz
50 g	2 oz	425 g	15 oz
75 g	3 oz	450 g	1 lb
100 g	4 oz	575 g	1¼ lb
150 g	5 oz	675 g	1½ lb
175 g	6 oz	800 g	1¾ lb
200 g	7 oz	900 g	2 lb
225 g	8 oz	1 kg	2¼ lb
250 g	9 oz	1.4 kg	3 lb
275 g	10 oz	1.6 kg	3½ lb
300 g	11 oz	1.8 kg	4 lb
350 g	12 oz	2.25 kg	5 lb

Liquid Measures The following chart lists some metric / imperial equivalents for liquids. Millilitres (ml), litres and fluid ounces (fl oz) or pints are used throughout.

METRIC	IMPERIAL
50 ml	2 fl oz
125 ml	4 fl oz
150 ml	¼ pint
300 ml	½ pint
450 ml	¾ pint
600 ml	1 pint

Spoon Measures Both metric and imperial equivalents are given for all spoon measures, expressed as millilitres and teaspoons (tsp) or tablespoons (tbsp).

All spoon measures refer to British standard measuring spoons and the quantities given are always for level spoons.

Do not use ordinary kitchen cutlery instead of proper measuring spoons as they will hold quite different quantities.

METRIC	IMPERIAL
1.25 ml	¼ tsp
2.5 ml	½ tsp
5 ml	1 tsp
15 ml	1 tbsp

Length All linear measures are expressed in millimetres (mm), centimetres (cm) or metres (m) and inches or feet. The following list gives examples of typical conversions.

METRIC	IMPERIAL
5 mm	¼ inch
1 cm	½ inch
2.5 cm	1 inch
5 cm	2 inches
15 cm	6 inches
30 cm	12 inches (1 foot)

MICROWAVE INFORMATION

Occasional microwave hints and instructions are included for certain recipes, as appropriate. The information given is for microwave ovens rated at 650–700 watts.

The following terms have been used for the microwave settings: High, Medium, Defrost and Low. For each setting, the power input is as follows: High = 100% power, Medium = 50% power, Defrost = 30% power and Low = 20% power.

All microwave notes and timings are for guidance only: always read and follow the manufacturer's instructions for your particular appliance. Remember to avoid putting any metal in the microwave and never operate the microwave empty.

Be very careful when heating liquids in the microwave as they can 'superheat'; i.e. the liquid's surface looks still but underneath there can be boiling bubbles that explode when the container is moved.

OVEN TEMPERATURES

Whenever the oven is used, the required setting is given as three alternatives: degrees Celsius (°C), degrees Fahrenheit (°F) and gas.

The temperature settings given are for conventional ovens. If you have a fan oven, adjust the temperature according to the manufacturer's instructions.

°C	°F	GAS
110	225	¼
120	250	½
140	275	1
150	300	2
160	325	3
180	350	4
190	375	5
200	400	6
220	425	7
230	450	8
240	475	9

Index